All Pro's GREATEST FOOTBALL PLAYERS

WAYNE COFFEY

SCHOLASTIC INC.
New York Toronto London Auckland Sydney Tokyo

ACKNOWLEDGMENTS

Special thanks are due the editors of *Sport* Magazine and Roger Goodell of the National Football League for their valuable research assistance.

ISBN 0-590-32918-9

12 11 10 9 8 7 6 5 4 3 2 1   9   3 4 5 6 7/8

Printed in the U.S.A.   01

DEDICATION

This book is for a beautiful rookie, Ronald Valentine Williams (world debut: December 29, 1982) and a beautiful friend, D.W.

TABLE OF CONTENTS

1. Earl Campbell 1

2. John Unitas 14

3. Kellen Winslow 28

4. Jim Brown 42

5. Dick Butkus 54

6. Roger Staubach 68

7. Walter Payton 82

8. Joe Namath 94

9. O. J. Simpson 110

10. Dan Fouts 124

EARL CAMPBELL

Earl Campbell, the hard-charging running back of the Houston Oilers, has made longer runs. And he has made more graceful and more spectacular runs. But if years from now football historians are looking for a film clip capturing the greatness of Campbell, they need look no further than a 15-yard rumble early in his career against the Los Angeles Rams.

"It was utter brute strength," marveled Andy Bourgeois, Houston's backfield coach, in describing the feat. "They finally stopped him right close to the goal line, but he ran over linebacker Isaiah Robertson, butted him to the ground, jumped over the top of him, ran through another guy. It took five or six guys to bring him to a halt. It was something to see."

"He's the toughest to try to bring down I've ever played against," Robertson said afterward. "He gets you off balance, then runs over you. If I had to tackle him every game, I'd make 'em double my salary."

Just about every defender who has ever gotten in the way of Houston's human freight train echoes Robertson's appraisal. Once, in a game against the Raiders, the Oilers had the ball just a yard from the Raider end zone. It was third down, and everyone on the planet knew Campbell would be getting the ball. Sure enough, No. 34 took the handoff, and just as he did, Jack Tatum, one of the hardest-hitting safeties in football, took a running start and bolted into the opening where Earl was headed. Perfectly positioned, Tatum braced for the touchdown-saving tackle. Seconds later, Tatum was on his back. Earl Campbell was in the end zone.

"In four years at Ohio State and eight seasons in the NFL," said Tatum, "I can't recall ever hitting anyone that hard without stopping him. I don't think any other back in the league could have scored after that hit."

It didn't take Earl long to show the NFL that he wasn't just "any other back." A Heisman Trophy winner at the University of Texas, he rolled up 4,444 yards in his star-studded tenure as a Longhorn. He was a Texas native, born and raised in the town of Tyler, and after one glimpse of what Campbell could do with a football tucked under his arm, the Oilers wanted to make sure he stayed a Texan. So the club shipped four draft choices and tight end Jimmie Giles to the Tampa Bay Buccaneers in exchange for the Bucs's top draft pick, which happened to be the first in the entire league. The five-for-one swap was one of the best deals the Oilers ever made.

Being the No. 1 pick in the country, Campbell burst into the pro ranks with much fanfare. A quiet, humble young man, he stayed away from boastful predictions or big talk about what he would accomplish. "I don't know what's going to happen," he said. "I'm confident I can play. I'm going to go out and do my best. That's about all I can do. If the good Lord wants me to have something, then I'll get it. But whatever happens, I'll always be a Longhorn, just like I'll always be from Tyler."

Earl had only one firm goal at the outset of his pro career, and that was to keep a long-standing promise to his mother. When he first enrolled at the University of Texas, he said, "I want to make enough money someday to build my mama a house so that when she goes to bed at night, she won't have to look through a hole and see the Big Dipper." The million-dollar contract Earl signed as a rookie made his dream a reality. The stunning new home was built on the same property where the family had been raised, with the Campbells' old house—a ramshackle little place—still standing beyond it. Earl wanted it that way; he never wanted to lose sight of where he came from.

Getting by was never easy for the Campbells. His father died when Earl was in fourth grade, leaving his mother the heavy burden of raising and supporting 11 children all by herself. Earl slept in the same bed with two of his brothers.

A decaying roof leaked whenever it rained. The family's sagging, run-down home lay on a dirt road outside of town. Only the income they collected from working in the Texas flower fields (Tyler is sometimes called "The Rose Capital of America") kept the Campbells from complete poverty.

By his own account, Earl was not exactly a model student early in high school. A linebacker on the varsity from his freshman year, his football talents were developing rapidly. So, too, were his bad habits. "By the time I was in high school, I was smoking a pack of cigarettes a day, doing a little hustling with a pool cue, gambling, drinking—the whole number. I didn't spend one minute thinking about the future. I thought one day I'd get out of school, get me a car, and bum around."

Fortunately, Earl's life did not stay off track for long. His bumming around resulted in his suspension once before a high school game—and in a severe reprimand from his strong-willed mother. "One day Mama got hold of me and she said, 'Earl, there's something in you that could be special, if only you'll let the real Earl come out.' She said one more thing. 'I'll work my fingers to the bone to bring you up, but I won't spend one dime to help you if you get in trouble with the law.' That shook me," recalled Earl.

"I straightened up."

With his act cleaned up, Earl began cleaning up on the football field. He once sacked the opposing quarterback eight times in a single game. He was big and fast and he loved to hit people, and finally a brainstorm came to his coach. What would it be like to have to stop a guy like that? wondered the coach. He decided to find out, so before Campbell's senior year, the coach asked him to switch to running back. Earl loved playing linebacker. He wasn't wild about the idea, to say the least. But he went along with it—and went a long way with it. He piled up more than 2,000 yards and his team captured the state crown, and before long, college coaches were beating down the door of the Campbells' little shack to convince Earl to attend their universities.

Coach Darrell Royal of Texas won the Campbell derby, and Earl went off to his big-time college football career. He had a painful adjustment at first, for reasons having nothing to do with the gridiron. He had never been away from home before. So he did battle with a bad case of homesickness. "He was the lonesomest kid I'd ever seen," remembered Royal. "He'd sit on the curb, facing Tyler, Texas, just the sorriest sight you'd ever see. I never knew when he might get up and hitchhike home and never return." Luckily, he never did. The only place

Earl went was right through every defense that stood in his way. Those who tried to stop him in college were only too happy to pass that burden on to the NFL. "A lot of people are thrilled that the Houston Oilers have Earl Campbell," said

Bill Yeoman, coach of the University of Houston. "Most of those people are college coaches."

They say first impressions are lasting, and that's especially true of Campbell. Trying to tackle him is not an experience that's easily forgotten. At 5-11 and 230 power-packed pounds, Campbell is as punishing a runner as has ever played. "He's awesome," concluded Jim Osborne, a defensive tackle for the Chicago Bears, after his first confrontation with Campbell. "Once I hit him in the leg, but you're taking your life into your hands when you do that. I think you have a better chance jumping on his back."

"I usually put two strips of foam rubber under my shoulder pads," added the Bears's safety Doug Plank, a fierce hitter himself. "After I looked at films of Campbell, I stuck three strips in there." Plank, as it turned out, got through the game intact. Chicago's other safety, Gary Fencik, didn't fare as well. "I hit Campbell nine times," said a woozy Fencik later. "That was one or two times too many."

"Earl Campbell is almost illegal," was the way Dwight White, a lineman with the Pittsburgh Steelers, put it. "When he hits that hole it's like a door slamming. Earl Campbell is like a Larry Csonka and O. J. Simpson combined." Indeed, much like the great Jim Brown, Campbell presents defenders with an impossible dilemma: He can just as easily run past them as he can run over them. When a pair of legs that are thicker than most tree trunks carry a 230-pound body at a 4.6 second clip in the 40-yard dash, it spells nothing but trouble for anyone who gets in the way. During a Monday night game against the Miami Dolphins in his rookie season, Campbell chewed up their line all game long with his hard-charging surges into the middle. Then, in the fourth quarter, Earl got the call to go wide. He took a pitch, eluded a tackler, turned the corner, and nobody laid a finger on him for the next 80 yards. He finished the game with 199 yards and four touchdowns.

That was the highlight of a sensational first season, the finest any rookie running back—including Brown and Simpson—had ever had. The team started being called the Houston Earlers, and for good reason. The bruiser in the backfield rang up 1,450 yards and 13 touchdowns. He was not only Rookie of the Year, he also was named the NFL's Player of the Year. Mike Nixon, director of college scouting for the Cleveland Browns, hailed the Oilers's gem as "the best in the league since Brown, and he could be the best ever."

O. J. Simpson could hardly disagree. "He's going to go farther than any back who has ever played in this league," Simpson said.

Campbell is well on his way to doing just that. He followed up his rookie exploits with seasons of 1,697 and 1,934 yards, and would've been a shoo-in to break O. J.'s mark of 2,003 yards if he hadn't missed eight quarters due to injuries. He became the first back ever to gain more than 5,000 yards in his first three seasons. A host of other records have fallen his way as well, including: most consecutive games, 100 or more yards rushing, season, 7; most games, 200 or more yards rushing, season, 4; most rushing touchdowns, season, 19; most games, 100 or more yards rushing, season, 11; most rushing attempts, season, 373.

Only the question of his long-term durability stands in the way between Earl and virtually every rushing record in the books. Because as much punishment as he doles out, he absorbs a lot, too. He's so powerful a runner that it seems he gets gang-tackled every time he touches the ball. And having 800 or 1,000 pounds of muscle hitting you 25 or 30 times a game, 16 times a season, has to take its toll even on a brute like Earl. "You can run right over people all the time in college," said Ken Riley, a cornerback with the Cincinnati Bengals, "but not in the pros. He's a great back, but he'll have to change his style to last ten years."

"He fights for everything he gets," added Jim LeClair, a Bengal linebacker. "It just remains to be seen how long he can last." Indestructible though he may look, Earl has learned that discretion sometimes is the better part of valor. Experience has taught him that sometimes it's better to go down or run out of bounds instead of plowing for an extra yard and letting four bodies crash into him from every direction. Sound judgment like that should keep Earl in the game that much longer.

No matter how long he lasts, Earl Campbell is content to let others worry if and when he breaks more records. "My goals are to play and be happy and do the best I can. If I stay healthy, the records will take care of themselves." This is one superstar who takes his status in stride. Constant media attention and adulation can give an athlete a swelled head in a hurry. Campbell wants no part of it.

"I don't want to be a big shot," he says. "Maybe other guys do, but not me. The important thing is to be yourself."

"Earl's different from any other great player I've ever known," said Bum Phillips, his former coach. "He seems to truly believe his teammates make him great. He always seems to be saying, 'I can only hope some day I'll be as good as you guys.' Earl doesn't say 15 words a week, and they're always the same two or three words: 'nice block,' or 'nice catch.' He does not say anything except to compliment a guy."

Whatever wonders he performs on the gridiron, it seems Earl always will remain the same—a quiet, gracious Texan who is as soft-spoken off the field as he is a thundering force on it.

A reporter once asked Texas coach Royal how Campbell had changed in his years as a Longhorn. Replied Royal, "The only difference in Earl Campbell as I remember him as a freshman and now is about 4,000 yards."

"You'd figure Earl would've come in here with a swollen head, winning the Heisman Trophy and all," said Carl Mauck, the Houston center, shortly after meeting his new teammate. "But he's as fine a human being as I've ever met."

Just about everyone who knows Earl Campbell describes him in similar fashion. But you'll pardon his opponents if they see him in a somewhat different light, having nothing to do with his quality as a person. "He's the greatest running back in football," said Cliff Harris, the former Dallas Cowboy safety. And what went through Cliff's mind when he saw the awesome No. 34 barreling toward him? "All you can do is close your eyes and hope he doesn't break your helmet."

EARL CAMPBELL

Year	Atts.	Yds.	Avg.	Tds.
1978	302	1450	4.8	13
1979	368	1697	4.6	19
1980	373	1934	5.2	13
1981	361	1376	3.8	10
1982	157	538	3.4	2
Totals	1561	6995	4.5	57

JOHN UNITAS

There are a lot of athletes who just seem destined for greatness, naturals from the time they leave the cradle. First as a kid on the block, then in junior high, high school, and college, they stand out at every level of competition. And nobody is surprised in the least when they wind up doing the same thing in the professional ranks.

There are those gifted few, and then there are those like John Unitas, who continually must fight and struggle to prove they belong. What's so special about Unitas is that he not only proved he belonged, he proved he was in a class by himself among NFL quarterbacks. If a writer ever made up a success story like Johnny U.'s, he probably would be criticized for creating a tale that was not believable. Sometimes real life is stranger than fiction.

Unitas's unlikely journey began in the Brookline section of Pittsburgh, where he grew up dreaming of becoming a professional football player. He blossomed into a local high school hero and hoped with all he had that he could continue his gridiron exploits in South Bend, Indiana, playing for Notre Dame. The Fighting Irish were famous for having football powerhouses, and Johnny had visions of becoming part of the school's rich football tradition. Unfortunately, a lot of other talented high school quarterbacks shared John's vision. With so many young men to choose from, the Notre Dame coaches elected to pass on Johnny Unitas. They told him he was too skinny to stand up to the punishment of big-time college football.

Disappointed, he enrolled at the University of Louisville. The school was far from a major football power, but John made the most of his years there, setting 15 records in his glittering career. The only problem was that hardly anybody noticed. He probably could've set 115 records and still not attracted national attention. Because no matter what he accomplished, the skeptics could always say, "Well, it's only Louisville. How good could the competition be?"

Unitas managed to get drafted by the Pittsburgh Steelers, but it wasn't until the ninth round, which meant that every team in the NFL had picked eight players before the Steelers got around to tabbing John. It also meant his chances of making the team fell somewhere between slim and none.

Knowing he was a long shot, the young quarterback was well aware he had to show his best stuff right from the start. He was determined to force the team to take him seriously. He worked diligently all through training camp and preseason, patiently waiting for his one big shot to show the coaches he was one ninth-round kid who could play the game. One preseason game passed, then another, and still John hadn't seen any action.

The regular season was rapidly approaching. Johnny didn't know what was going on. How could they decide on him without seeing how he could perform in a game? John kept his mouth shut and continued making the most of his practice time. Finally, Johnny was called in by the coach, who told the youngster flat out that he wasn't good enough to make the grade in the NFL and handed him a ten-dollar bill for bus fare home. A shattered John Unitas stuffed the bill in his shirt and hitchhiked home. With a wife and small child to support, he had to save money wherever he could. "The grim thing about it," said Unitas later, "was that the Steelers never gave me the opportunity to play."

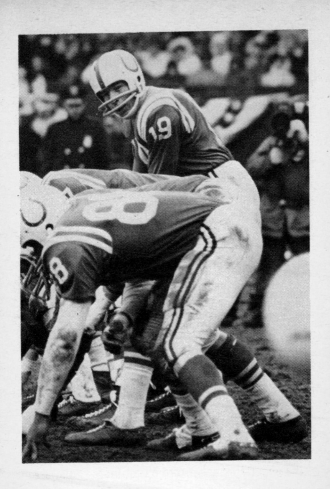

Shut out of the NFL, the young signal-caller turned to the GPL—the Greater Pittsburgh League. He had a construction job to earn some real money and got a quarterback job to stay involved in the game he loved in hopes of getting a shot from some other team in the big time. One thing was for sure, though—the GPL was not the big time. It was a semipro league, but the playing conditions were worse than most Little Leagues. The pitted fields were rocky and rubbly, and maybe 100 fans would show up for a big game. Unitas's compensation for playing quarterback for the Bloomfield Rams was $3 per game. Clearly, he wasn't in it for the money.

"I would've played for nothing," said John. All he wanted was to stay sharp in the event that some NFL club needed quarterback help. He wasn't holding his breath.

As it happened, Don Kellett, the general manager of the Baltimore Colts, was quarterback shopping in the winter of 1956. Kellett was sifting through old NFL waiver lists when he came across the name John Unitas. The general manager called Weeb Ewbank, the Colts' coach, and Weeb called Frank Camp, who was John's coach at Louisville. Camp gave his former pupil high marks as a quarterback, and not long after, Unitas got the surprise of his life—a phone call from the general manager of the Baltimore Colts, asking if he would like to try out. Johnny dashed off to Baltimore. The Colts liked what they saw, and when the 1956 NFL campaign opened, John Unitas was the Colts's backup quarterback.

John didn't expect to see much playing time because the Colts had a well-established starter in veteran George Shaw. But situations have a way of changing dramatically in pro football, a sport in which injuries are commonplace. Unitas barely had a chance to sit down before Shaw got racked up and was sidelined early in the year. Ewbank called on his raw recruit to step into a game against the Chicago Bears.

Moments later, John dropped back and let loose with his first NFL pass. It was caught, and it went for a touchdown. The trouble was that the guy who caught it was J. C. Caroline, who played for the Bears. Matters never got any better for the shell-shocked rookie that day. He fumbled once himself and, being unfamiliar with the plays and his new teammates, botched two hand-offs resulting in two more fumbles. The Colts got thumped. Nobody felt worse than John Unitas, who had about the most nightmarish debut any quarterback could have.

"I went down to the locker room," Colts' owner Carroll Rosenbloom said later. "John was never one to show his emotions. But he was sitting in front of his locker. He still hadn't taken off his uniform. His head was hanging between his legs so that all you could see was the top of his crew cut. I walked over and got him under the chin and lifted his head up. I said, 'Now look, John, that was not your fault. You haven't had an opportunity to play and no one is blaming you. You're not only going to be a good one in this league, you're going to be a great one.' "

Even then, as an inexperienced 23-year-old suddenly thrust into the spotlight, Unitas showed he had the competitiveness and mental toughness of a champion. Just one week after his horror show against the Bears, John came back and sparked a Baltimore victory, firing two touchdown passes in a 28–21 decision. After that, he seemed to get better every week. By the end of the year, he'd established an NFL record for a rookie by posting a completion percentage of 55.6.

Rosenbloom was impressed. Ewbank was impressed. And in 1957, the entire NFL was impressed. Unitas gave them no choice. With a year's experience under his belt, John's performance far exceeded his or anybody else's wildest expectations. He threw for 2,550 yards, while connecting on 57.1 percent of his passes for 24 touchdowns. Unitas was the sensation of the league. "Who is this guy?" fans wondered. "Where did he come from?" In Pittsburgh they were asking a different question: "How in the world did we ever let him get away?" Only the Steeler coaches knew for sure, and they weren't too eager to talk about it. Johnny U.'s fairy-tale year concluded with being named the NFL's Most Valuable Player. Not too bad for a fellow who two years earlier had been doing his passing in the Pittsburgh sandlots.

The fairy tale did not end there—not by a long shot. This was one young star who wasn't going to have a good year or two and then fade into obscurity. With Unitas at the helm in 1958, the Colts got off to their best start in years. Their masterful young quarterback had them in the thick of the race for the Western Conference crown. But then misfortune struck.

Looking to pass in the Colts' sixth game of the season, Johnny was corralled by a lumbering lineman, who hurled him to the ground. The fierce tackle left Unitas writhing on the stadium turf, fighting the piercing pain of a punctured lung and three cracked ribs. Nobody knew how long he would be sidelined, but most people figured a month, probably more. The timing could not have been worse as far as John and the Colts were concerned. Fighting for a title, the team could ill afford to be without the services of its star quarterback.

"Pain is part of the game," John would often say, and he was one to know, having suffered numerous serious injuries in his 18-year career. "You get used to it," he said, and he must have meant it. Because only three weeks after being decked, Unitas got taped up and returned to com-

bat. The massive crowd at Baltimore's Memorial Stadium went wild when No. 19 trotted onto the field. Unitas responded by performing as though he'd missed only a couple of downs. He uncorked a TD pass on his very first throw, and the rest was easy, as the Colts galloped to a 34–7 rout of the Los Angeles Rams. Baltimore went on to capture the conference title and braced for a championship showdown against the awesome New York Giants.

The Colts got off to a rousing start. Unitas connected with running back Lenny Moore for a 60-yard touchdown, and the quarterback's razor-sharp air game steered the Colts to another score. Baltimore surged to a 14–3 lead at half-time.

But just when the Giants appeared doomed, they came storming back. Inspired by the heroic performance of its defense, which stopped the Colts cold on four cracks at scoring from the three-yard line, New York suddenly had Baltimore on the run. Two TD's lifted the New Yorkers to a 17–14 lead, and their defense seemed to play more fiercely each time they came on the field. The pass rush on Unitas was constant. Johnny led the Colts out for a final shot at tying or winning. Only 1:56 remained. The Colts were on their own 14-yard line. They had an awful lot of field to cover, and not much time to do it.

"Now we find out what stuff we're made of," rasped Johnny to his teammates. And with that he went to work. He fired to Moore for an 11-yard pickup. He rifled a 25-yard bullet to split end Raymond Berry. Calling all the plays at the line of scrimmage—the Colts had no time for huddles—Johnny stepped into the pocket, scanned the field, and drilled one to Berry again, this for 16 yards.

Time was ticking away. Unitas barked out the signals and set up quickly. Once more, Berry worked his way into the clear. Johnny delivered the pigskin right on target. Twenty-one yard gain. The Colts were at the Giant 7. Only seven seconds remained. Unitas had done his job magnificently. Passing as though it were a practice drill and not the waning moments of a championship match, he had advanced his team almost the entire length of the field. The Colts' fate lay with kicker Steve Myhra, who came on to attempt a game-tying field goal. The ball snapped into the holder's hands, and Myhra stepped up and struck the ball solidly. It sailed through the uprights. The game moved into overtime. The first team to score would be the winner.

After a Giant drive stalled, the Colts got the ball on their own 20. Johnny calmly connected with fullback Alan Ameche for a first down, but then the New York defense stiffened. They swarmed in on Unitas, nailing him for a 12-yard loss. It was third down and 15 to go. The Giants charged hard again, knowing John would be passing. Protected in the pocket, Unitas spotted Berry open downfield, but quickly realized the end was short of first-down yardage. Johnny waved him to go deeper, and Berry dashed downfield. Unitas cranked the arm and let it fly. Complete! The 20-yard advance pushed the Colts to the New York 42.

Playing with the savvy of a 15-year vet, John

brought the Colts to the line and alertly spotted that the Giants had aligned in a pass-defense formation. The quarterback shouted out a new play, faded back to dupe the Giants, then tucked the ball into Ameche's midsection. The fullback took off all the way to the New York 19. Having used his master mind, John went back to his master arm, with good result. Two more completions propelled Baltimore to the doorstep of victory— just three yards away from the end zone. John called another play, took the hike, and handed off deftly to Ameche. The powerful back steamed into the middle, slipped through a hole, and barreled into the end zone. Touchdown! The Baltimore Colts were NFL champions. Johnny Unitas, who played as though he didn't have a nerve in his body, was named the game's Most Valuable Player. It was no wonder. He hit on 26 of 40 passes for a record 349 yards.

Over his career, Unitas made a habit of coming through with his best performances when it counted the most. He set NFL marks for completion percentage (62.9) and passing yardage (1,177) in championship games. He also walked off with another MVP trophy in 1959, when he tormented the same Giants with an encore effort, firing two TD's and rolling up 264 yards to spark a 31–16 triumph.

A host of other records fell his way, too. Consistently among the premier passers in the game, Unitas was the first quarterback to throw for more than 40,000 yards in his career; had the most games with 300 or more yards passing, 26; the most seasons leading the league in TD passes, 4; and most consecutive games with a touchdown pass, 47, a remarkable feat that rivals Joe DiMaggio's 56-game hitting streak in baseball. That Fran Tarkenton eventually surpassed a good many of John's accomplishments in no way diminishes the greatness of the one-time sandlotter. He was twice voted the NFL's Most Valuable Player (1964 and 1967) and honored as the league's Player of the Decade for the 1960s. Unitas's crowning achievement came shortly before his retirement in 1973, when he was named the greatest quarterback in the NFL's first 50 years.

Great as he was, Johnny Unitas never seemed comfortable receiving all the acclaim and attention his brilliant career warranted. "I just like to play football and win games," he said. He was extraordinary at both.

JOHN UNITAS

Year	Atts.	Comps.	Pct.	Yds.	Tds.	Ints.
1956	198	110	55.6	1498	9	10
1957	301	172	57.1	2550	24	17
1958	263	136	51.7	2007	19	7
1959	367	193	52.6	2899	32	14
1960	378	190	50.3	3099	25	24
1961	420	229	54.5	2990	16	24
1962	389	222	57.1	2967	22	23
1963	410	237	57.8	3481	20	12
1964	305	158	51.8	2824	19	6
1965	282	164	58.2	2530	23	12
1966	348	195	56.0	2748	23	24
1967	436	255	58.5	3428	20	16
1968	32	11	34.4	139	2	4
1969	327	178	54.4	2342	12	20
1970	321	166	51.7	2213	14	18
1971	176	92	52.3	942	3	9
1972	157	88	56.1	1111	4	6
1973	76	34	44.7	471	3	7
Totals	5186	2830	54.6	40,239	290	253

KELLEN WINSLOW

Time was running out on the San Diego Chargers. Their backs were against the wall. They had to do it now, or let the big one slip away. With each passing tick of the clock, the Chargers' hopes of pulling it out got dimmer and dimmer.

Finally, with just seconds remaining, the Chargers went for it. And they wound up with one of the biggest scores in the franchise's history.

Any clues about what we're talking about here? A playoff game? An American Football Conference championship match? A key regular-season battle with an archrival? They're all good guesses. But they're all wrong. We're talking about the NFL draft.

The draft? How could that be? What about the ticking clock and the big score? Well, this was a draft that had all that and more for the San Diego Chargers.

Kellen Winslow: the San Diego Superman

Braintrusts from all 26 NFL teams—general managers, scouts, coaches, and others—had assembled for the 1979 college draft. Slated to make the 20th selection of the first round, the Chargers sat by nervously as name after name was announced. The team's draft people felt helpless. They knew who they wanted, but they also knew there was practically no chance he would be available by the time it was their turn to pick. Thus far, their efforts to swing a trade had not been successful.

Still, all was not lost. Because the man the Chargers coveted, Kellen Winslow, a showstopper of a football player from the University of Missouri, remained untabbed. Ten picks were made—Winslow was still available. Then came No. 11 and No. 12, and neither one picked San Diego's man.

It was time for the No. 13 selection, which belonged to the Cleveland Browns. Each team is allotted 15 minutes to make its pick. Quickly, the Chargers' draft team huddled with the Browns', headed by Tommy Prothro, Cleveland's director of personnel. Cleveland had no need for a tight end, and the Chargers knew that. San Diego offered two draft choices in exchange for the Browns' No. 13 slot. Prothro mulled it over. Time was running very short. A decision had to be made or the choice would be forfeited. Prothro and

Eugene Klein, San Diego's president, went back and forth right up to the wire. Finally, Prothro agreed to the swap. Whoops of joy went up in the San Diego camp. The Chargers had their man.

"We were very surprised Kellen hadn't been picked yet," Klein revealed later. "We had him rated number one in the country. We went through a long process to get him, and we ended up doing it with about six seconds left in our allotted 15 minutes."

What about Winslow? What made the Chargers so bent on snagging him? Sure, he'd been an All-American at Missouri. And he put some very respectable numbers on the board in his years there, catching 71 passes for 1,089 yards, a 15.3 yard average, and 10 touchdowns. But in this case, the numbers don't begin to tell the story. Because with Kellen Winslow, the proof is in the looking.

He is an awesome physical specimen. He is 6-5½ and weighs 245 pounds, and if you're thinking those are dimensions more befitting a lineman, you're not far from the truth. But he moves like anything but a lineman. A rare combination of power and grace, he can flatten a defender with a straight-ahead plow or escape him with fakes and finesse. One incident at Missouri perfectly captures his dazzling combination at work. "This defensive back raced up to hit me," recalled Winslow, "and he bounced off and went straight to the ground. I stopped and looked at him for what seemed about five minutes. Then I started running again." Nobody caught him.

"We thought he had fabulous potential for the pros," raved Eugene Klein. "We had a tremendous need for a young tight end because Bob Klein was nearing the end of his career. Our scouting reports said that Kellen had size, speed, great hands, and toughness. He's certainly lived up to all our expectations."

If the Chargers desperately wanted Winslow, the feeling was very mutual. "What worried me about the draft," said Kellen, "was what team I'd go to, and whether I'd be able to accomplish all the things I wanted with them. The predictions had me going to Buffalo, Cincinnati, or Chicago—somewhere cold where they didn't throw the ball that much. But I knew it would be harder for me to accomplish my goals in those places, so coming to San Diego was a dream come true. And when I saw the players they had—Dan Fouts and John Jefferson and Charlie Joiner—I knew anything was possible.

"If I hadn't gone to San Diego," Winslow went on, "I don't think you'd ever have heard of Kellen Winslow. I might be weighing 275 right now and playing tackle. But I'm just lucky to be with a team that's committed to the pass."

Nor would we ever have heard of Kellen Winslow if it weren't for a man named Cornelius Perry. Perry was a physical education teacher and football coach at East St. Louis High School. Winslow had little interest in football during high school. Indeed, his career nearly ended before it started. Kellen went out for the squad as a sophomore. He lasted all of two days. That's all he needed of the backbreaking twice-a-day practices to decide there were more pleasant ways to spend his time.

"I wasn't too crazy about the sport," acknowledges Winslow now. "So I just went back to being Kellen the student. I also went out and got a job after school with United Parcel Service. I thought it was a good opportunity to make some money and prepare myself for the future. And I played on the chess team in my spare time."

The more Perry thought about a 6-4, 185-pound kid playing chess, the more he became committed to convincing young Kellen to get back out on the gridiron. "He was a natural athlete," said Perry, "that was easy to see. But he lacked confidence. I had to make him see that there were better things ahead."

"I thought about it for awhile," told Winslow, "and I decided it was something I wanted to see if I could do. Besides, the coach also was really concerned about my future. He told me I had a lot of ability and I was wasting it. I'm glad I listened to him, or else I'd probably still be at United Parcel and going to college at night. I put my trust in him, and I ended up here in the NFL." The Chargers are sure glad he did. The rest of the NFL is not.

Winslow's impact was immediate and immense. He'd barely stepped into the Chargers' blue and gold when his teammates began calling him Super Rook. His speed, power, moves, and gluelike hands made him an instant favorite of San Diego quarterback Dan Fouts. He led the team in receiving in the first part of the season, snaring 25 Fouts aerials for 255 yards and a couple of touchdowns. But just as Winslow's rookie year was hitting high gear, he absorbed a wicked shot and broke his leg. His season ended then and there.

Undaunted, he picked right up in 1980 where he left off in 1979. He wound up the campaign with 1,290 yards, nine touchdowns, and a record-breaking 89 receptions. Previously the mark for catches by a tight end was 75. He was named to the all-pro team and became the most feared pass catcher in the game. "The guy has ability, size, and something else," said Joe Gibbs, who was the Chargers' offensive coordinator before moving to Washington and leading the Redskins to the Super Bowl in 1982. "He's probably the smartest football player I've ever seen outside of a quarterback. For all this tremendous ability, his intelligence is what really sets him apart. I've never seen anybody learn as fast as he does."

NFL defenders learned fast, too—that there was almost no limit to what Winslow could do on the football field. As one observer commented, "How are you supposed to defend a guy who can out-jump, outrun, out-muscle, and out-finesse everybody else out there?" The question answers itself: You can't.

Kellen's abilities are so diverse that the Chargers use him much differently than they would a normal tight end. In a single game, he often lines up as tight end, running back, slot back, wide receiver, and as a man in motion. The opposition gets confused because it doesn't know where he might go or what he might do. In essence, he has created a new position. Nobody quite knows what to call it. "If you have to label what I am," said Kellen, "just call it receiver." Most people just call it awesome. "Probably no other player in football can break a defense in so many unique ways," was the way one writer put it.

Neither the Los Angeles Raiders nor the Miami Dolphins need to be convinced of that. Late in the 1981 season, the Chargers headed north to play the Raiders (then in Oakland) in a critical

AFC West showdown. San Diego had been blown out in its two previous games. It badly needed a victory to keep its flickering playoff hopes alive. Winslow took matters into his own massive hands in a way only he could. He caught 13 passes,

Winslow blocks for teammate Eric Sievers.

which is outstanding in itself. But even more remarkable is that five of those catches went for touchdowns, a feat that tied a 31-year-old record. Winslow's heroics paced the Chargers to a 55–21 shellacking of the Raiders. "We seemed to pick up right there behind Winslow's performance," said San Diego coach Don Coryell.

The Chargers went on to win the division and defeat the Buffalo Bills in the first round of the playoffs. Their next challenge was a showdown with the Miami Dolphins in the conference semifinals. If there were any fans across the country who somehow didn't know about Kellen Winslow, they found out about him on that memorable afternoon. Many people think the game was the greatest in NFL history. Winslow was among the biggest reasons why.

It looked like anything but a great game as it unfolded. San Diego surged to a 24–0 lead before the end of the first quarter. By half-time, Winslow had gathered five passes for 55 yards, and the Chargers seemed well on their way to the AFC championship game.

The Dolphins had other ideas. Not only did they refuse to roll over, they scratched and clawed their way into a 24–24 deadlock in the third quarter. From then on it was nothing but high drama in the Orange Bowl.

The Chargers regained the lead later in the

third quarter, when Winslow bolted into the clear, eluding the swarm of Miami defenders that shadowed him all afternoon, and hauled in a 25-yard touchdown pass. The score stood at 31–24, but the Dolphins were equal to every challenge. Every time it seemed the Chargers would put the game away, the Dolphins fought back to tie. With only seconds to play in regulation time, the score was tied at 38–38, and Miami was in field goal position. A quick-thinking Coryell sent Winslow in to play defense. The coach reasoned that a 6-5 leaper such as Winslow had to be the best bet on the team to block the kick. The snap was made, the ball was set down, and up went the kick. Up went Winslow, too, soaring over everyone else on the field. *Thwack!* He timed his leap beautifully and batted the ball to the turf. The Chargers had life.

In overtime, the Chargers moved in for a field goal of their own. Miami had no Kellen Winslow to block it. Rolf Benirschke's kick sailed right through the uprights, and the Chargers were winners. Winslow didn't see the moment of triumph, however. Blocking on the play, he collapsed facedown on the turf, exhausted, cramping severely, and he remembered, ''ready to cry.'' Two teammates had to help him off the field.

He had richly earned the escort. Winslow was far and away the leading man in the four-hour, three-minute spectacle. Apart from his game-saving field-goal block, he collected a playoff record of 13 passes for 166 yards and a touchdown. And he did it in a humid, 80-degree heat with two and sometimes three Dolphins hitting him in every way imaginable. The Dolphins knew they had to stop Winslow to win the game. They tried everything they could short of sticking half the team on him, and nothing worked.

Indeed, no team in the NFL has yet to devise a way to contain Winslow. It's not likely they will. Already being hailed by many as the greatest tight end ever, Winslow led the league or conference in receptions in each of his first three full seasons. It's no wonder he's talked about with awe.

On a *Monday Night Football* telecast featuring the Chargers, he was referred to as the "All-Universe" tight end. *Sport* Magazine has called him "the most powerful offensive weapon in the game today." Says Dan Fouts, the man who throws the ball to him and knows better than anyone the amazing feats Kellen routinely performs, "I've never seen anyone with his athletic ability. I think he may be the best football player in the game, at any position."

He can block like an interior lineman. He can run like a halfback or a fullback, depending on what's required. According to Fouts, "He can throw a football 80 to 100 yards." Of course, he can catch passes as well or better than anyone ever has. Is there anything Kellen Winslow can't do on the gridiron? Don Shula, coach of the Dolphins, hasn't found it.

After Winslow devastated Miami in the memorable playoff game, a reporter asked Shula what he thought of the San Diego tight end. "When you think about Winslow," replied the veteran coach, "you think Superman."

KELLEN WINSLOW

Year	Recepts.	Yds.	Avg.	Tds.
1979	25	255	10.2	2
1980	89	1290	14.5	9
1981	88	1075	12.2	10
1982	54	721	13.4	6
Totals	256	3341	13.0	27

JIM BROWN

"Give everybody in the line an ax."

That was the way Alex Karras, a standout defensive tackle for the Detroit Lions, once proposed to stop Jimmy Brown. Certainly no legal method had ever worked. One look at the bruising fullback revealed why. Rock hard at 230 pounds, his massive torso rippled with muscles. He was strong and lean, with barely an ounce of fat on him. He could run over the roughest, toughest lineman and run past the most fleet-footed defensive backs. The word "unstoppable" is overused in the sports world, but it's the best way to describe Jim Brown.

He played all of his nine seasons with the Cleveland Browns, leaving behind almost as many records as he did tacklers. Maybe the ultimate tribute to the Browns' famed No. 32 is that nearly 20 years after he retired, he remains the standard by which all running backs are judged. "There's not been anyone close to him since he left the game," said John Wooten, who was an all-pro himself as a guard for the Browns, and now is a scout for the Dallas Cowboys. "I mean not even close. That may sound like a put-down of some of the great backs in the game now, but it isn't meant to be. It's just that there was only one Jim Brown. He was that rare."

Brown was indeed an incomparable athlete, and even as a schoolboy, he wasted little time proving it. He had every coach at Manhasset High School on New York's Long Island begging Jim to play for his team. Brown started on the varsity football team as a 14-year-old, and by the time he became a senior, he was averaging the unheard-of figure of 15 yards every time he carried the ball. He was a standout lacrosse player and wasn't too shabby at basketball, either; he averaged 38 points a game for the school team. He was named to all-state teams in football, basketball, and track, and became good enough in baseball to attract offers from the New York Yankees and the Boston Braves. Small wonder that one Manhasset coach declared, "Name the game, and he'll play it like a pro in 48 hours. He could be an all-American in anything from tiddlywinks to football."

The scholarship offers poured in during his senior year before Jim decided to attend Syracuse University in upstate New York. He progressed slowly in the first part of his career, and badly wanted more time on the field to show what he could do. But when he had his first big game, powering for 150 rushing yards as a junior, Brown was sure he'd be inserted into the lineup fulltime. He found out otherwise. Two games after his sterling performance he was back on the bench, and seething. "That made me so mad I saw fire," said Brown. "And in the next practice scrimmage, I left first-string tacklers all over the field and ran for four touchdowns in five plays." The Syracuse coaches finally seemed to realize the gem they had on their hands, and Brown became a regular, going on to finish second in the East in rushing yardage.

In his senior year, Brown gave a dazzling clue of the greatness to come. He bruised and battered defenders all season long, and then, in his final regular-season game, he single-handedly destroyed archrival Colgate. The powerhouse scored six touchdowns, rolled up 197 yards on the ground, and figuring in his seven extra-point conversions (he handled Syracuse's kicking duties as well), personally accounted for 43 points.

Sparked by its brilliant running back, Syracuse lost only one game all season, and was chosen to play in the Cotton Bowl against Texas Christian. Brown had fashioned quite a reputation for himself in the East, but it wasn't until he performed in the national spotlight of a bowl game that the rest of the country came to appreciate his towering abilities. In a hard-fought 28–27 loss, Brown was clearly the best player on the field, running for three touchdowns and 132 yards. Among those convinced that Jimmy Brown was a blue-chip professional prospect was Paul Brown, coach of the Cleveland Browns. Paul drafted Jim, and for the next nine years, Cleveland's football fans were sure glad he did.

Often NFL rookies go through a period of adjustment in which they must get accustomed to their team's system and to the sophisticated professional defenses of their opponents. Jimmy Brown's period of adjustment lasted for about as long as his first carry. He steamrolled over just about every defense that got in his way. And by year's end, he'd amassed a league-leading 942 rushing yards, nine touchdowns, and a superb average of 4.7 yards per carry. He also set a record by powering for 237 yards in a single game and carried the Browns to the Eastern Conference championship.

The rookie sensation had a tough act to follow in his second year. He knew very well that every team the Browns would face would coordinate its entire defensive game plan to stop him. But no matter what elaborate plots were hatched during the coaches' brainstorming sessions, the simple fact was that nothing worked. Because even when Brown was contained perfectly, he could still carry half a team on his back. "All you can do to stop him," said all-pro linebacker Sam Huff of the New York Giants, "is grab hold, hang on, and wait for help." Before the help came, Brown piled up a league record of 1,527 yards in his sophomore season, averaging an astonishing 5.9 yards per carry. His 18 touchdowns also earned him NFL scoring honors with 108 points. In a single game in 1959 against the NFL's champion Baltimore Colts, Brown blasted through for five touchdowns, igniting Cleveland to a stunning 38–31 upset.

Sunday after Sunday, season after season, Brown was the most awesome offensive force the NFL had ever seen. He made a mockery of the annual competition for the NFL rushing crown. From 1957 through 1961, the top rusher in the league was Jimmy Brown. Not a bad percentage: five seasons, five rushing titles. Even he couldn't do better than that. It's one record many experts feel will never be surpassed.

The only problem was that the fans were so used to Jim winning the title that when he finished second in 1962, some Cleveland rooters were upset and lamented that Brown was not the runner he used to be. They chose to ignore that Brown played the season with a painful injury to the arm he used to ward off tacklers. "I'm no Superman," said Jim in response to the whispers of criticism. "I had a good season—not a great one, though. Do I have to lead the league *every* time for it to be a good year? I don't like to boast, but I think I'm as good as anyone in this league as an all-around offensive player."

Any fan foolish enough to think Brown was anything but the best was left with heaping amounts

Brown plus a blocker meant big trouble.

of egg on the face in 1963. All Brown did was power his way for 1,863 yards—farther than a mile, farther than anybody had ever run before. He did it by averaging 6.4 yards every time he carried. He also tallied 12 touchdowns and played the hero's role in one of Cleveland's biggest games of the year. The Browns were down by 13 points to the powerful New York Giants, the defending conference champions, when they cut loose their one-man wrecking crew. On one play, Jim flared out of the backfield, corraled a screen pass, and bolted through the Giant defenders for a dazzling 72-yard touchdown. With the game on the line in the fourth quarter, he ripped right up the middle for a 32-yard score. Cleveland eked out a 28–27 decision.

Brown's performance that season was even more remarkable when you consider that each team only played a 12-game schedule, as opposed to the 16-game schedule of today. That means Jim averaged better than 150 yards per outing. "The man could have had 2,000 yards that year if he'd played four quarters every Sunday," said John Wooten. The reason he didn't play a full game each week was because he usually was so devastating that the game already was out of hand and there was no sense in keeping him in the game. Absolutely nobody was surprised when he was named the NFL's Most Valuable Player.

After that Brown played only two more seasons and captured league rushing honors in each. That ran his total to eight titles in nine years. But Brown already had earned enough accolades for ten players; he deeply wanted to win a championship for the team. In 1964, he got the chance. On the strength of Brown's 1,446 rushing yards, Cleveland won the conference title and squared off against the heavily favored Baltimore Colts in the NFL championship game.

The Colts had the best defense in the league. But the Browns had a peerless weapon. It was no contest. Jim racked up 114 yards on the ground and forced the Colts to become so bent on stopping him that Cleveland quarterback Frank Ryan had plenty of opportunity to hurt Baltimore elsewhere. The final score was 27–0. Jimmy Brown, rushing champion, was now an NFL champion, too.

"The team championship is the most important thing," said Jim. "That's what I wanted, what I needed. The individual glory and the records are okay. But if you're involved in a team game, you want to be a part of the best team."

One season and one more rushing crown after Brown became a champion, he announced his retirement from football. The news jarred the football world as much as his hard-charging style had jarred hundreds of tacklers. There was no

Gang tackling was the only way to stop Jimmy Brown.

logical reason for him to quit—at least on the surface. He'd performed brilliantly in the 1965 season, picking up another 1,544 yards, and showed no signs of slowing down. Jim often had said he didn't want to hang on and keep playing once his skills started to falter. But he was far from that point; he was still at the very peak of his game.

"It's a shame he had to quit so soon," said Wooten glumly. Brown, for his part, did not make a big deal of his retirement. He'd begun pursuing an acting career—he appeared in the film *The Dirty Dozen*, among others—and felt he'd accomplished all he had set out to do.

The numbers Jim Brown left behind are staggering. He set so many records that even the statisticians had trouble keeping track of them. The great O.J. Simpson has since overtaken Brown in some categories, yet a great many more of Jim's feats remain unsurpassed. Among those are: most yards gained, career, 12,312; most touchdowns, career, 126; most seasons leading league in rushing, 8; most seasons, 1,000 or more yards rushing, 7; most games, 100 or more yards rushing, career, 58; most rushing attempts, career, 2,358; highest average gain per carry, career, 5.22 yards. If they'd had a category called "Most Punishing Runner, Ever", you can bet that would have been alongside the name Jim Brown as well.

Nobody can say with certainty that Jim Brown was the greatest runner in NFL history—even if the vast majority of those who saw him play have no doubt about it. Statistics are not the final measure of any athlete.

One statistic, however, does provide a clue to the greatness of Jim Brown. And that is his average of 5.22 yards per carry. This number means that over his nine-year career, every time he plowed into a defense he averaged a gain of better than 5 yards. No other runner has come close to duplicating that figure for his career. What makes Brown's feat that much more remarkable is that he accomplished it against defenses that usually *knew* he would be carrying the ball and aligned themselves accordingly.

Forewarned is supposed to be forearmed, but not against Jimmy Brown. That's why unstoppable is the only way to describe him.

JIM BROWN

Year	Atts.	Yds.	Avg.	Tds.
1957	202	942	4.7	10
1958	257	1527	5.9	18
1959	290	1329	4.6	14
1960	215	1257	5.8	11
1961	305	1408	4.6	10
1962	230	996	4.3	18
1963	291	1863	6.4	15
1964	280	1446	5.2	9
1965	289	1544	5.3	21
Totals	**2359**	**12,312**	**5.2**	**126**

DICK BUTKUS

For a long time whenever a team played the Chicago Bears, its offensive players were sure their eyes were playing tricks on them. That's because everywhere they looked, there seemed to be a huge No. 51 staring them in the face. A sweep to the left—No. 51 darts over and shuts it down. A pass over the middle—No. 51 drops back and bats it away. A run up the middle—No. 51 throws aside a few blockers and slams the ballcarrier to the ground. *Just how many No. 51's do the Chicago Bears have?* opposing players often wondered.

It may have seemed like a half-dozen, but in reality the Bears had only one No. 51: Dick Butkus. And he was everywhere he needed to be on the field. His position was middle linebacker, and from the moment he made his first bone-crunching tackle, the Bears knew they had a very special talent. "The day Dick showed up, I knew I was out of job," said Bill George, the man Dick replaced as the anchor of the Chicago defense.

Butkus joined the Bears in 1965, a two-time All-American from the University of Illinois. He was one-half of probably the greatest duo of draft picks ever made. In a matter of seconds, with back-to-back first-round choices in the 1965 NFL college draft, Chicago coach George Halas drafted two of the NFL's all-time greats—an offense-wrecker and a defense-wrecker. The defense-wrecker was Gale Sayers, a fleet-footed running back from the University of Kansas who instantly became the most dazzling and dangerous offensive weapon in the league. The offense-wrecker was Butkus.

A 6-foot-3, 245-pound mountain of muscle, Butkus did not have Sayers's grace or agility. But his job wasn't to elude people, as Sayers's was. His job was to hit them. And by the time a string of serious injuries ended his career in

1973, he had done that job better than any middle linebacker in NFL history.

Butkus's impact on the Bears was immediate—and amazing. In one season, his fierce tackling and relentless rampaging transformed the league's second *worst* defense into the league's second *best* defense. Manning a post that one coach described as "the toughest position to play well," he constantly kept the offense preoccupied just by his very presence. Where would he go next? Who would he hit? Would he blitz? Would he position himself in a way to fool them into trying one kind of play, and then just as quickly move back and ruin it? Butkus could—and often did—alter an offense's game plan all by himself. It's precisely what he wanted to do —keep them guessing, throw them off guard, make them so confused that they would get away from what they do best. "The best kind of defense," Dick once observed, "is the kind that forces the offense to react." Butkus was a master at it. Once, playing against an inexperienced quarterback, he charged right up to the line of scrimmage, menacing the signal-caller into thinking he would be blitzing. The quarterback hurriedly scooted back and rushed a pass over the middle—the spot vacated when the middleman blitzes. But Butkus never charged, dropped back a few steps, and made an easy interception.

Butkus bats down a John Unitas pass.

He made his opponents react in other ways, too, such as with pure terror. "There are guys who make tackles, and there's Dick," said Doug Buffone, who played alongside the Bears' iron man in the linebacking corps. "He's a mauler. I hit hard, but no matter how hard I hit, I don't hit *that* hard."

"When Dick is on the other side of the line of scrimmage, glaring at you with those boiling eyes, it makes you wish you could change places with the equipment boy," said Brian Piccolo, the late running back. And Piccolo only had to square off against Butkus in practice. Imagine how he terrorized opponents in games. Fran Tarkenton, who played against Butkus for years and somehow survived to become the most prolific passer in NFL history, knew only too well.

"You just can't believe a guy hits that hard," said Fran in his book, *Tarkenton*. "You just can't seem to fool him away from a play, either. . . . I think Dick Butkus is the greatest football player I've ever seen. Certainly the toughest.

"He was so great that he could take a group of average football players and make them play better than they knew how to play," said Tarkenton. The reason, Tarkenton said, was "because they respected him so much they were scared of what he would do to them if they didn't play.

"Whenever you played the Chicago Bears you were aware of Dick Butkus. . . . You knew that any time you ran or passed successfully you would somehow have to escape him. He was going to make an interception or he was going to chase a play forty yards. . . . He kept his team in a frenzy every game. He was the most dominating single player I've ever seen in a football defense. He had the kind of temperament that made him want to engulf the whole offense by himself."

The Butkus temperament was shaped from an early age. Growing up with eight brothers and sisters in a tough Chicago neighborhood, he learned quickly that he had to be rugged to make it in the inner city. Kids in the neighborhood learned quickly that Dick Butkus wasn't a good guy to mess with.

Chicago is a fanatical football town, and Dick caught the fever early. "In the fifth grade," he recalled, "I knew what I was going to be—a professional football player. I worked hard at becoming one, just like society says you should. It said you had to be fierce. I was fierce. Tough. I was tough."

Few who played against him would disagree. Indeed, his unbridled intensity and rugged style of play earned him more than his share of unflattering labels in his career—"Animal," "Subhuman," "King Kong," "Gorilla" were just some of them. You get the idea. So did Dick, and it didn't bother him at all. "I play the game the way I think it should be played," he said. "And if they think that's animalistic, well. . . . Still in all, I must be doing something right for them to be calling me names."

Toughness may be the first quality that springs to mind when the name Butkus is mentioned. But to think that's all he had going for him would be grossly mistaken. When he first came into the league, a lot of people took one look at his thick, burly body and figured he couldn't be very mobile. No linebacker that big, the logic went, could possibly play effective pass defense. Butkus wasted no time proving otherwise, intercepting five passes in his rookie season.

"I once looked him off a pass," remembered Norm Snead, a former quarterback for the New York Giants. "I faked and faked, and he kept sliding over and over to where I was looking. Then I suddenly turned and threw to the other side of the field. That man was there to knock the ball down, and I think it was a time when his leg was bothering him, too."

"I've never been timed in a 40-yard dash, and I couldn't care less," said Dick. "They always said I was weak on passes because I was the biggest and weighed the most. . . . I wonder if I got down to 235 and was the same weight as everyone else if they would say the same thing.''

Appearances, Butkus's opponents found out quickly, can be very deceiving. ''He looks fat, clumsy, and awkward,'' was the way Tommy Prothro, former coach of the Los Angeles Rams and San Diego Chargers, described him. ''But he kicks the devil out of everybody. And if you pass, he's there, too.''

In addition to his deceptive agility, Butkus was one brute who had brains to match. Opponents continually were astounded that someone who played so fiercely could also be so smart at the same time. Possessed of a remarkable ability to read formations and anticipate how plays would unfold, he was the hardest linebacker in the league to fool. ''Butkus has to be the smartest middle linebacker I've ever seen,'' raved Abe Gibron, a coach with more than 25 years in the game.

Tarkenton once marveled at Dick's ''technical brilliance.'' But to Butkus, it was nothing more than the result of a lot of hard work—spending countless hours reviewing game films and constantly expanding and refining his knowledge of the game. ''The first couple of years, I played on physical ability alone,'' revealed Butkus. ''As the years go by, you learn what experience means, just watching a team and knowing what they'll go to, being able to read patterns, knowing where to go yourself.

"At the key moment," he went on, "the instant of the snap, I somehow know most of the time how the flow pattern will develop. It's all there in the backdrop. I stare right through the center and the quarterback, right through their eyes. I watch for the keys, and they are very tiny keys. Tiny little twitches of the shoulders and their heads and their feet and their eyes. There's just this split second, before it all starts to move, when you'd put those keys together and you know—or you'd better know—how it's going." Not bad brainwork for a brute. It was this kind of concentration that enabled Butkus to be in the middle of practically every play.

A Monday night game against the Minnesota Vikings typified Butkus's brilliance. One of the top teams in the league, the Vikes did their best to run their plays away from the middle and exploit other areas of the Chicago defense. But it didn't work, as Butkus sparked a Bear upset with his mind as well as his muscle. He did his usual yeoman job anchoring the defense, making five tackles, a fumble recovery, and an interception. But he also devised two shrewd play calls in kicking situations. One time the Bear quarterback, holding for the field-goal kicker, faked the defense by picking up the ball and dashing for a first down. Later, the Bears faked a punt, completely fooled the Vikings, and wound up with a 23-yard pass completion for a first down. Both tricks came on a tip from Butkus. "The Vikings have a great kick rush," said Dick afterward. "I studied their films all week." Then he came up with a couple of ways to make the Vikings' aggressive charge work to the Bears' advantage. The Vikings rushed so hard that they went right past the forward-moving Bear offense.

Perhaps the only part of Butkus that could match his toughness was his pride. From the time he began playing the game, he was driven to be the best. He would tirelessly pummel himself into peak physical condition. He would practice longer and work harder than other players. He would play with pain when another player might not. "Every time I play a game," he said, "I want to play it like it was my last one. I could get hurt, and that would be it for keeps. I wouldn't want my last game to be a lousy one. My goal," he went on, "is to be recognized as the best. When they say middle linebacker, I want them to mean Butkus."

When he was healthy, Butkus's status as the

league's premier linebacker was unquestioned. An all-pro in each of his eight full seasons, he twice was named as the NFL's top defensive player. But following a serious knee operation in 1970, some experts doubted whether Butkus could ever be the same ferocious and dominant force again. One writer predicted that Mike Curtis of the Baltimore Colts would assume Butkus's throne as king of the middle linebackers. How did Dick feel about the article? Suffice it to say it's a good thing for the reporter that he never had to step on the field against No. 51.

"When I saw that story," told Butkus, "I sat down and had a long talk with my knee. I told my knee all about it. All during camp, whenever I felt like taking it easy, I'd remind my knee of Curtis."

A lot of people paid a painful price for the writer's prediction that year, as Butkus played with a fury that was remarkable even for him. "If there's anything an offense hates to see more than Dick Butkus," wrote one observer, "it's Dick Butkus mad." In the Bears' first preseason contest against the Steelers, Butkus destroyed whatever doubts anybody had about him. Pittsburgh tested "Mr. Mean" on the second play of the game, sending running back John Fuqua straight up the middle—Butkus territory. Seconds later there was a heavy thud, and Fuqua was flat on his back, courtesy of Dick Butkus, who met him head on with a bone-crushing tackle. By the time the game was over, Butkus had two interceptions, forced a fumble with a devastating hit, made seven tackles, and generally made life miserable for the Steelers.

The Bears won the game, but even with the mighty middleman breathing fire into their defense, that was one thing the team didn't do very often during the Butkus years. Only twice during his career did Dick play on a winning team. He liked losing about as much as he liked quarterbacks who tried to show him up. But even though he never got close to playing in a championship game, his intensity never wavered. His way of coping with the frustration of defeat was to take it out on the other team. "I look over at the other team warming up," said Dick, describing his pregame routine, "and I look for the guys who are smiling or fooling around or acting silly. Then I say to myself, 'He thinks he's going to have it easy today, huh?' That sets me off, and the more I watch, the hotter I get. When the game starts, I'm ready to tear people apart."

Opposing players rarely had it easy when Dick Butkus was prowling around on the other side of the scrimmage line. "I have never seen a player with greater desire," said his coach, Abe Gibron.

"He's a once-in-a-generation ballplayer." Which is why, for as long as he played, the position middle linebacker did, in fact, mean Butkus. And why there always seemed to be more than one No. 51 on the field for the Chicago Bears.

ROGER STAUBAUCH

Things could hardly have looked gloomier for the Dallas Cowboys. The Pittsburgh Steelers had just struck for two touchdowns in 17 seconds, and the explosion left them with a commanding 35–17 lead with seven minutes to play. Super Bowl XIII seemed all but over.

On the sidelines, the Steelers were loose and relaxed. Handshakes were exchanged, and a number of battle-weary players wore the proud and happy look of champions. "I wouldn't pop the champagne just yet if I were the Steelers," cautioned one veteran sportswriter. "They shouldn't forget that Dallas has the Miracle Worker on its side."

The writer was referring to Roger Staubach, the Cowboys' quarterback. Miracles are not the work of mortals, but Staubach came closer than anyone to performing them on the football field. Time and again over his 11-year career as Dallas' field general, he pulled victory from the clutches of defeat. Before nearly 80,000 fans in the Orange Bowl and some 75 million TV viewers across the country, he was trying to work his magic once more.

Staubach led the offense on. He wasted no time getting them in gear. He rifled a couple of pinpoint passes for clutch gains and scrambled for a key 12-yard pickup, and in a matter of minutes, the Cowboys were on the Pittsburgh 7-yard line. Spotting an open target in tight end Billy Joe DuPree, Roger delivered on the mark and the big receiver rumbled into the end zone. Staubach had moved his team 89 yards in eight plays. Only 2:27 remained. Dallas trailed 35–24, still needing two TD's to pull it out.

Kicker Rafael Septien came on and squibbed the onside kick that everybody knew was coming. A wild scramble for possession ensued, and when the officials sorted out the pile of bodies, Dallas' Dennis Thurman was the man with the ball. Out came Staubach again. "Our guys were dancing around, saying how great it was," said Terry Bradshaw, the Pittsburgh quarterback. "But I knew it wasn't so great, because the game was far from over."

The Cowboys started from their own 48. Staubach faded back and fired a 22-yard bullet to end Drew Pearson. Three plays later, he connected with Pearson again, this one good for 25 yards. The ball lay on the Pittsburgh four. The Steelers' premature celebration on the sidelines was no more. Roger took the snap and dropped back. Butch Johnson broke swiftly into the end zone. Timing the play perfectly, Roger flipped a short aerial and the end hauled it in. Touchdown! Septien's conversion made the score 35–31. Dallas fans were delirious.

Just twenty-two seconds were left. Septien booted another squibber, only this time Pittsburgh recovered it. Dallas had no time-outs. The Steelers ran out the clock and breathed a huge sigh of relief. They knew they had just barely escaped. They also knew they had just witnessed one of the most heroic quarterbacking performances in Super Bowl history. Staubach couldn't pull this one out, as he'd done so many times before for the Cowboys. But that doesn't diminish the wonder of what he did in those final minutes with pressure mounting with each tick of the clock. Overall, he completed 17 of his 30 passes for three touchdowns and 228 yards. He also ran four times for 37 yards. He was brilliant. He just ran out of time.

Staubach had an uncanny knack for delivering his best efforts in the biggest games. Some competitors seem to wilt under intense pressure; Roger thrived on it. "I swear he has ice in his veins," remarked one observer after witnessing a Staubach-led comeback. Said another, "Noth-

"Roger the Dodger" cuts into the open.

ing throws the fear of God into coaches like Roger Staubach trotting onto the field in the final minutes of a close game.''

And there was good reason: Staubach engineered 23 fourth-quarter come-from-behind triumphs over his career. Even more remarkable is that 14 of them came in the final two minutes of play or in overtime. Any doubters of Roger's penchant for the dramatic should go directly to Coach Bud Grant and the Minnesota Vikings. That's who bore the brunt of probably Staubach's most famous feat of all.

Under a minute remained in a 1975 NFC playoff showdown. The Vikings were clinging to a 14–10 lead, and the Cowboys were clinging to a shred of hope. Staubach was looking at a bleak fourth-and-long situation from deep in his own territory. The game had come down to this; it was over if he didn't get a first down. Working out of the shotgun formation, Staubach took the snap and scanned the secondary, which was dense with Minnesota's purple jerseys. Finally, he spotted a target and winged a deep sideline pass to Drew Pearson, who hauled it in at midfield, just inches from the sideline.

Moments later, Staubach dropped back once more. The Vikes were laying back in a prevent defense, willing to concede a medium-yardage pass in order to stop the long one. Pearson streaked down the sideline, accompanied, seemingly, by half the Minnesota team. Staubach wound up and cut loose with a deep, high-arching bomb. Following its flight closely, Pearson pulled up, came back a step, and seized the ball out of heavy traffic. A couple of loping strides and he was in the end zone. Only seconds remained. The Cowboys—and Roger Staubach—had done it again.

Roger's road to superstardom was an unusual one indeed. Early in his career, some people doubted how good a quarterback he could be or even if he was good enough to stay in the league. Nobody questioned his athletic ability; he had a strong arm and was a sensational runner. What had people wondering was the layoff.

He began playing football for Purcell High in Cincinnati, where he emerged as an outstanding halfback. Few things gave the fleet-footed youngster more pleasure than eluding tacklers and running with the football. It came as a heavy blow to Staubach when his coach told him he didn't want him as a runner anymore. Instead, the Purcell coach wanted Roger as his quarterback.

How did Roger feel about the switch? "I don't want to play quarterback," he said. "I love to run with the ball, and on this team the quarterback isn't allowed to run very much." That all changed once young Staubach became signal-caller. He got to run, he got to pass, and by the time he was a senior, he got flooded with scholarship offers. He decided he wanted to attend the U.S. Naval Academy, where, before any student—even a star athlete—is enrolled, a difficult entrance examination must be passed.

Roger didn't achieve the required score and was faced with the choice of forgetting about Navy or taking the exam a second time. Ever the battler, Staubach opted for the hardest route; he went to another school for a year, studied hard, and passed the Navy exam on his second chance.

He was a prize pupil on the gridiron. Early in his second year, he came off the bench against Cornell and sparked a Navy victory, running for two touchdowns and passing for a third. He became an instant hit in Annapolis, where his fellow midshipmen took to calling the dashing quarterback "The Navy Destroyer." Even then, Roger was at his peak when it counted the most. In the Middies' yearly classic with Army, he directed a high-powered attack that enabled Navy to cruise to a 34–14 triumph.

It wasn't long before he began attracting nationwide attention. One of the greatest running quarterbacks in college football history, he captured the coveted Heisman Trophy in his junior year at the Academy. For anyone else, that probably would've meant all kinds of attention and a big pro contract. This Heisman winner, however, would not be moving right into the NFL, and that's where the layoff entered the picture. Naval Academy graduates are obligated to serve for four years after their studies are finished.

Few NFL teams are that patient. Four years is an awfully long time to be away from the game. There was no guarantee he could play pro ball after that kind of hiatus, assuming, of course, that he still wanted to. It wasn't until the tenth round of the 1963 NFL college draft that the name Roger Staubach was called. The choice was made by the Dallas Cowboys, who figured it was worth it to use such a low pick for a talent like Roger. What did they stand to lose?

Four years came and went, and Staubach showed up at the Dallas training camp, a rusty quarterback in search of a job. It wouldn't be easy, he knew that. Even though he'd kept himself in good condition, Roger was well aware that playing quarterback required a feel for the game and an instinct about what to do that could only return to him with time.

He worked doggedly in camp and earned a spot on the team as the backup to Craig Morton. He was happy to have overcome the first obstacle in his return to football, but a fierce competitor like Staubach wasn't going to be content merely to be suiting up. After two years as Morton's

**Staubach hands off to running back
Calvin Hill.**

understudy, Staubach was growing restless. He
wanted to be the No. 1 quarterback and that was
all.

Coach Tom Landry had been watching Staubach's steady improvement, and as the 1971 season opened, the Dallas coach elected to go with
a two-quarterback system. Neither had a right to
the job; whoever was more effective in a given

game would play. But complications set in when the Cowboys got off to a sluggish start. Landry's plan didn't seem to be working. He had to make a decision, and he did. Roger Staubach was the Dallas Cowboys' new No. 1 quarterback. The coach's move was a huge relief to Roger, who felt as though he spent as much time glancing to the sidelines to see if Morton was coming in than he did reading opposing defenses.

"Now if I make a few mistakes I'll still be in there," said Staubach. "I won't be walking a tightrope anymore. This way I'll come through a winner."

Roger never gave Landry any cause to regret the decision. In fact, the former Navy Destroyer made his coach look like a genius. The Cowboys reeled off seven straight victories to close the season, picked up two more in the playoffs, and went all the way to the Super Bowl, which pitted them against the Miami Dolphins.

Amid all the pregame discussion and hoopla, some people questioned whether Staubach, with less than one full season of full pro quarterbacking behind him, would be able to withstand the nerve-racking pressure of playing in a Super Bowl. A man expressed that opinion to Commodore Paul Borden of the United States Navy, who knew Roger from their days at Annapolis. "This game is a big game," said the officer, "but I'm not sure how much bigger it is in comparison to the Army-Navy games when Roger was so much younger. Every midshipman, every officer, why, every admiral in the fleet—they were all on Roger's shoulders. But he thrives on pressure. He seems to respond to it perfectly.''

The commodore's words turned out to be prophetic. In the most important game of his life, Staubach came through in a big way. He passed for 119 yards on 12-for-19 accuracy against the Dolphins's vaunted ''No-Name Defense,'' and that was good for two touchdowns and one Most Valuable Player award. Engineering a 24–3 triumph, Staubach showed the football world that he was well worth the four-year wait.

He kept on showing them the rest of the decade. Under Roger's able direction, the Cowboys remained among the NFL elite throughout the 1970s, winning four NFC titles and two Super Bowls. Staubach himself was consistently outstanding. He rarely had the staggering statistical games—say, 400 yards passing, five touchdowns, and the like. But that was only because the Dallas offensive system wasn't built to produce such numbers. All Roger did was make very few mistakes, come up with game-winning feats at the most crucial times, and, of course, win.

He led the league in passing four times and laid claim to all kinds of club and league records.

He completed more Super Bowl passes (61) than any other quarterback. When he retired in 1979, he left with 1,685 completions in 2,958 attempts, 22,700 yards, and 153 touchdowns. Those numbers add up to the highest quarterback rating (83.5) of any man in NFL history.

About the only wrong Staubach ever committed—at least to Cowboy loyalists—was to retire. His final season may well have been his best; he hit on 58 percent of his throws for 27 touchdowns and only 11 interceptions. He was the best passer in the league. It hardly seemed like a time to retire.

But Roger had made his decision, and it was final. At an emotional farewell press conference, he said he had "a gut feeling" that it was time to exit. "I want to spend more time, more quality time, with my family," he said. Roger didn't say so, but those who knew him well figured his proud and competitive way entered into the decision as well. There was no way a man like Staubach could hang on and keep playing, just for the sake of playing. Being the best meant everything to him. So why not bow out that way? His only wish, he said, was "to be remembered as a pretty darned consistent performer."

Staubach, of course, was all that and much, much more. To say Roger was pretty consistent is like saying the Sahara Desert is kind of dry.

He would never say it, of course—it wasn't his style—but year in and year out, Roger Staubach was consistently the finest quarterback of his time.

"When you think about the Cowboys' success in the '70s," said all-pro safety Charlie Waters, "you've got to look directly to Roger. He was the epitome of a competitor, the leader of leaders."

"I've got nothing but superlatives for a guy who is truly what an all-pro quarterback represents to me," added middle linebacker Bob Breunig. "He's one of those people who has all the priorities set up. He has a great sensitivity for people and gives so much to people. No one will ever know how much, really."

Indeed, Staubach is one of those rare athletes who has been praised as much for his kindness and humility off the field as his tremendous skill on it. He commands respect in a way few people can. "There's no question," said Dallas president Tex Shramm, "that Roger Staubach is this country's greatest sports hero today, maybe of our time. He is unique in that his following spans all age generations."

All in all, he didn't do too badly for a tenth-round draft choice, did he?

ROGER STAUBACH

Year	Atts.	Comps.	Pct.	Yds.	Tds.	Ints.
1969	47	23	48.9	421	1	2
1970	82	44	53.7	542	2	8
1971	211	126	59.7	1882	15	4
1972	20	9	45.0	98	0	2
1973	286	179	62.6	2428	23	15
1974	360	190	52.8	2552	11	15
1975	348	198	56.9	2666	17	16
1976	369	208	56.4	2715	14	11
1977	361	210	58.2	2620	18	9
1978	413	231	55.9	3190	25	16
1979	461	267	57.9	3586	27	11
Totals	2958	1685	57.0	22,700	153	109

WALTER PAYTON

A few years back the Minnesota Vikings were preparing for a game with the Chicago Bears. Coach Bud Grant was running a game film of the Bears to clue in the Vikings on what to look for and to help them formulate a defensive game plan. In one sequence, the film showed a dazzling display by Walter Payton, whose cuts, fakes, and artful dodges left defenders strewn all over the field. Awed by what they'd seen, the Vikings burst into a round of spontaneous applause.

Coach Grant had never seen anything like his players' response. Usually top athletes maintain a professional cool toward one another's performance; they know they are all extremely gifted, and to an extent, they take greatness in stride. ''It gives you an idea of what the rest of the league thinks about Walter Payton,'' said Grant. ''He has that quality both as a football player and a human being. The pros just love the guy.''

The Bears have loved him from the moment he showed up in 1975, a first-round draft pick out of Jackson State, where he established the NCAA career scoring record of 464 points. He did everything but sell game programs at the small, all-black Mississippi college. He was the team's punter, placekicker, and sometimes even its passer; he completed 14 of 19 tosses for four touchdowns during his college career. "One day he came out to the Bears' practice in square-toed kicking shoes," remembered Neill Armstrong, former Chicago coach. "He said, 'I can kick off.' I said, 'I know you can, but I don't want to see you with your leg up in the air.' He'd probably kick it out of the end zone and we wouldn't have to cover, but I don't want to see anyone get a shot at him."

There seems to be no limit to Payton's gridiron skills. A sure-handed receiver, he's so good at catching passes that in practice he'll often race downfield and catch 50-yard bombs with one hand. He's also a devastating blocker who is capable of flattening defenders as though he were a burly offensive lineman. In one game, he blocked Al Baker, the Detroit Lions's fine defensive end, and flipped him head over heels. "Just caught him right," said Payton.

"I'm sure glad he doesn't play free safety,"

said Chicago's free safety Doug Plank, who figured he'd be looking for work if that were the case. One former Bears coach discussed how Payton was one of the finest tacklers on the team. Whenever an interception was thrown, he always seemed to be the guy who would make the stop.

"That kid would be the greatest one-man show ever seen," exclaimed Jim Finks, Chicago's general manager, early in Payton's career. "He could punt, kick off, kick extra points, kick field goals, pass, catch, block. A phenomenal athlete."

And a phenomenal runner, his best attribute of all. At 5-10½ and 204 pounds—comparatively small by pro football standards—he is one of the strongest, most punishing runners in the league. He can bench press 390 pounds and leg press more than 600. One of his teammates said Walter was the strongest guy on the Bears, linemen included. "He's equivalent to a 6-2, 240-pound back in structure," said Finks.

"You wouldn't think such a little dude like that would have so much power," said Richard Harris of the Seattle Seahawks. "I hit him once and I thought I had him stopped, and he almost ripped my shoulder off."

"To me," added Norris Thomas, a cornerback with the Miami Dolphins, "he's a combination of Jim Brown and Earl Campbell. He's got power to run over people and the speed to run by people.

That kind of guy is a threat any time he has the ball. We have to keep him within the pocket, making him run from tackle to tackle instead of going outside. You just can't give him the option to pick holes and go where he wants."

Is there a way to contain him? "Maybe barbed wire," joked another cornerback, Bobby Bryant of Minnesota. "I figure it's similar to trying to rope a calf. It's hard enough to get your hands on him, and once you do, you wonder if you should have." Neither Bryant nor any of his Viking colleagues had much luck laying a hand on Walter on November 20, 1977.

On that day, the "Dancing Bear," as they sometimes call him, broke loose for 275 yards rushing, an NFL single-game record. For some backs that would be a pretty good total for half a season. He wound up the year with the staggering sum of 1,852 yards, the fourth-highest figure in NFL history.

"He's what I call one of the insane runners," said O. J. Simpson, who held the old rushing mark for a game (273), "the kind who can make the moves without having to stop and think."

"He always makes the correct cut because he has great depth perception," commented his backfield coach, Fred O'Connor. "He always knows the leverage, the angle a defender has on him. He never tries to anticipate the angle. He sees it and feels it. Consequently, he's able to make his cuts at full speed. That's the difference between a great back and a lot of guys who make the right cuts but have to come under control to make them.''

It's obvious that Payton does, indeed, have a feel for the game because he hasn't even been playing it very long. Up until his junior year in high school in Columbia, Mississippi, he did his playing on the drums instead of the football field. He was in the school marching band and performed in jazz-rock bands. "He'd come through the house, beating on anything he could put his hands on—the tables, the bed, whatever," recalled Walter's mom Alyne. "All he did was drum. It was when he'd start early in the morning that it was really hard on me.''

Walter left the football to his older brother Eddie, who was the star of the school team and who also has played in the NFL. According to the younger brother, his mom wasn't wild about having two football-playing sons. Mrs. Payton tells a different story.

"Eddie is a real talker," she said. "But Walter has always been quiet, sort of off by himself. Eddie used to tell Walter all sorts of things about football—what to do here, how to do this and that—and I think Walter sort of resented it. And when they'd sit and watch games on TV, Eddie

was always running outside to practice things he'd seen, but Walter never did that. He'd just sit and watch, and that was all.''

The year after Eddie graduated, Walter went out for the team. ''He wasn't really excited about football,'' said his mother, ''but as it turned out, he was a star right from the beginning. In his very first game he had a 61-yard touchdown run.''

He has been doing it ever since. After an injury limited him to 679 yards in his rookie year in 1975, Payton dashed for 1,390 yards in his second year and has never looked back. He's piled up so many yards—better than 10,000 through his first eight years—that some players have taken to calling him ''Real Estate Man.'' For five years in a row, he was the top ground-gainer in the National Football Conference. Barring an injury, he's a solid bet to eclipse Jim Brown's all-time rushing mark of 12,312 yards.

The ultimate team player, Walter's success has invited all kinds of questions and comparisons concerning the feats of the other all-time great backs, men like Gale Sayers, who also played for Chicago; Brown; and Simpson. Such talk is the part of the game he likes the least.

''I don't want to make anybody forget about anybody,'' he says emphatically. ''. . .I really don't enjoy comparisons. I just want to be Walter Payton. I want to leave the game with people saying, 'Now that Walter Payton, he was a team player.' "

"Believe it or not, it really doesn't mean a thing," Payton said about the records. "Sure you look at those records and say you wouldn't mind accomplishing that. But working toward it is more important. It's like climbing a mountain. You struggle, and there are lots of tricky things in the way. But once you get there, the only thing left is the other side of the mountain."

His individual accomplishments mean little to him. For virtually his entire career, he has heard comments such as, "Payton carries the Bears" or "Chicago's a one-man team." And he doesn't care for it one bit. "If there're no linemen in front of me, there's no *me*. I'm not a team, I'm a team player. I never felt like I carried the Bears, or could. . . . It takes ten other guys to win a game—and ten other guys to spring me loose on a long run or get me an extra yard."

The Dancing Bear is good to his word. More important than talking like a team player, he acts like one. He hits the blocking sleds as often and as hard as the most unheralded lineman. Some runners take a rest when they're not carrying the ball, but not Payton. He blocks with the same zest with which he runs. "It's important to me to just be one with my teammates," he said. Talk to his teammates and coaches, and there's no doubt he has succeeded. Late in his second year, Payton broke the 1,000-yard mark for the first time. Lionel Antoine, an offensive tackle, rushed over to him. "I grabbed him and told him I loved him," said the 6-foot-6 lineman. "There isn't anyone on the team who works harder."

"He makes us feel like we gained the 1,000 yards," added guard Revie Sorey, which is just how Walter thinks about it. "They're the ones who do the work," he said. "My running doesn't indicate how well they block." To show his appreciation, he gave each lineman a gold watch at the conclusion of that first 1,000-yard effort. His inscription was, "Thanks for the 1,000 yards." He also gives them the ball whenever he scores a touchdown, letting them spike it and take a turn in the spotlight. It's easy to see why Backfield Coach O'Connor once said, "I've never been so impressed with any young man as I am with this guy. . . . He has a perfect attitude."

Another name that has been hung on Mr. Payton—he has almost as many nicknames as he has moves—is "Sweetness." And it's not just because of his kind, unselfish ways. It's also because watching him run with the football—juking, weaving, and darting through a tangle of defenders—is a sweet sight to behold. Says one rival coach, "The guy has more moves than a checker game. He can stop on a dime—and I mean *stop*—and be off again at top speed in a blink of an eye.''

"The man is armed and dangerous," said Alan Page, the former Viking great who spent many a frustrating afternoon chasing No. 34. ''If he doesn't beat you on one play, you have that hollow feeling that sooner or later he'll leave you for dead on another one.''

''If you're off balance, he'll run over you," added Ed O'Neil of the Detroit Lions. "He's strong, fast, he has balance, great moves, and intelligence. If you're too slow, he'll outrun you, too.''

By any name—the Dancing Bear, the Real Estate Man, Sweetness, or just plain Walter— his career has been one of the longest-running hits ever on the NFL stage. The irony is that the humble young man is a victim of his own greatness. He has spent a career trying to downplay his own achievements, but the closer he draws to Brown's legendary yardage record, the more accolades and attention have been focused on him. Payton can do wonderful things with his marvelous, muscle-packed body. But one thing he can't do is control what people are saying or thinking. At the head of the Walter Payton fan club are two guys named O.J. Simpson and Jim Brown. At the close of a routinely brilliant season, O.J. sent Payton a telegram bearing this message: CONGRATULATIONS. BEFORE YOUR CAREER IS OVER, THE RECORDS I OWN WILL BE GONE AND FORGOTTEN.

All Brown said was, "I've never seen a runner with better instincts. The NFL won't see many like him."

Which is why Coach O'Connor was moved to say, "God said he was going to make a football player, and He made Walter Payton." And why Walter Payton is worth applauding—no matter what team you're on.

WALTER PAYTON

Year	Atts.	Yds.	Avg.	Tds.
1975	196	679	3.5	7
1976	311	1390	4.5	13
1977	339	1852	5.5	16
1978	333	1395	4.2	11
1979	369	1610	4.4	16
1980	317	1460	4.6	7
1981	339	1222	3.6	8
1982	148	596	4.0	1
Totals	2352	10,204	4.3	72

JOE NAMATH

People from coast to coast were talking about it. In playgrounds, office buildings, schools, and homes, football fans of all ages could hardly believe what they had heard. It was a prediction heard 'round the sports world. To one observer, it also was "probably the stupidest thing an athlete has ever said."

A little background: Super Bowl III was rapidly approaching. The NFL representative had won the first two games by blowout proportions. Every indication was that this one would be more of the same. The Baltimore Colts, after all, were being hailed as one of the greatest teams in NFL history. They finished the regular season with a 13–1 record, the best mark since 1942, when the Chicago Bears were 11–0. They completely embarrassed a powerful Cleveland Browns team, 34–0, in the NFL championship match. Over the season, the Colts rang up an average of close to 30 points per game, while yielding only 10. To many, the Baltimore defensive unit was the finest ever assembled.

Opposing the Colts were the New York Jets, who enjoyed a fine season but who looked like David compared to the Colts' Goliath. Nobody, it seemed, would give the New Yorkers even a fighting chance. "If you thought the first two Super Bowls were one-sided," said one account, "wait till you see this one." Another advised, "The Jets should seriously consider not showing up." "If the Jets win, I'll eat a frog," said a caller to a radio phone-in program.

At least one person felt differently, and it was he who created all the stir. His name was Joe Namath, and he happened to play quarterback for the New York Jets. He was tired of the way his team was being insulted and scoffed at by the media. The quarterback strongly believed another opinion needed to be aired. So he aired it. Holding court to a batch of reporters poolside at a Miami hotel, Namath dropped his bombshell. "We'll win," he said matter-of-factly. "I guarantee it."

The newspeople were agog at the statement, maybe the brashest prediction ever made by a football player. And Namath wasn't finished. "There are at least four quarterbacks in our league who are better than Earl Morrall," he said, referring to the fine Baltimore signal-caller, who was the NFL's leading passer and Most Valuable

Player that year. "There's Daryle Lamonica, John Hadl, Bob Griese, and myself. In fact," Joe went on, "you put Babe Parilli (the Jets's backup quarterback) with Baltimore, and Baltimore might be better. Babe throws better than Morrall."

The Colts were livid. The cocky kid from the big city had thrown down the gauntlet, and they couldn't wait to pick it up and jam it into his oversized mouth. Namath, the enraged Baltimore players vowed, would be eating a lot of humble pie come January 12, 1969. A whopping three-touchdown favorites, the Colts were hoping to win by six touchdowns, just to teach the New York quarterback a lesson.

It didn't quite work out that way. The only eating Namath did that day at the Orange Bowl was of the vaunted Baltimore defense. Between his ingenious play-calling and pinpoint passing, Joe had the Colts crossed up the entire game. He completed 17 of his 29 passes for 206 yards, masterfully engineering a 16–7 New York triumph, one of the biggest upsets in sports history. For his efforts, Namath was awarded the game's Most Valuable Player award. "Namath was fabulous," exclaimed Weeb Ewbank, the Jets's coach. "He didn't make a bad call."

"Namath did everything," said Baltimore Coach Don Shula.

"I hope they eat their pencils and pads," were

Joe's words for all those media people who ridiculed his prediction. "This has to be the most satisfying win in my life."

Joe and his Jets may well have surprised everybody by what they did on the field. But this is for sure: Joe didn't surprise anybody by being in the spotlight. He never strayed very far from it in his 13-year stint as one of the premier quarterbacks ever to play.

In 1963, the Jets, then called the Titans, were a hapless and bankrupt team desperately in search of new talent, a new identity, and new fans. In 1965 they got all three. How? By signing a heralded quarterback from the University of Alabama named Joe William Namath.

He made a huge media splash long before he ever threw his first professional pass. His $400,000 contract, the most ever given to a rookie in any sport, made him an instant sensation. So, too, did the way he had about him. *Webster's New World Dictionary* defines *charisma* as "a special quality of leadership that captures the popular imagination and inspires allegiance and devotion." For Jets' fans, its definition was simply "Joe Namath." As Sonny Werblin, the team's owner and the man who was paying him the money, said, "He has the presence of a star. You know how a star lights up the room when he comes in? Namath has this quality."

Part of it was the Namath look. Ruggedly handsome, he had twinkling blue-gray eyes and a chiseled face that was framed by a shaggy shock of long, dark hair. Then there was his lifestyle, which tended toward the fast and fancy. He lived in a posh New York apartment building, where his furnishings included a round bed and a white llama rug. When he wasn't there, chances were he was patronizing one of the city's chic nightspots, usually—to the delight of the newspaper gossip pages—with an attractive young woman at his side. He simply had a flair and style that were all his own. He wore long hair when crew cuts still were the order of the day in the NFL. He grew a Fu Manchu mustache when almost everyone else was clean shaven, and then shaved it off when he was offered $10,000 to do so in a television commercial. He wore white shoes when the rest of the league was wearing black, and no matter where he went, he was determined to be his own man. Once, in an Italian restaurant, the waiter came over and suggested he order clams *oreganato*, *fettucine alfredo*, and other elaborate dishes. "I'll have spaghetti and meatballs," said Joe. The waiter urged Joe to try one of the delectable house specialties. "I'll have spaghetti and meatballs," repeated Joe, and that's what he got.

Super Joe engineers the Super Bowl upset of the Colts.

He was exactly what the struggling, young AFL needed. With Namath around, the Jets, the league, and Joe himself were never far from the headlines. It may not always have been exactly the kind of publicity the AFL wanted, but there's no question it played a huge part in getting more and more people into the seats.

But for all his engaging ways, the biggest reason of all for Namath's mystique was the way he played quarterback. It's a position that suited him perfectly, and the one he always wanted to play. In the beginning, the main problem was simply getting the chance. As a high school sophomore in Beaver Falls, Pennsylvania, he wasn't even included in a special preseason training camp. Fifty players were invited, but not young Joe. His game experience that season consisted of one play.

The youngster did not give up. He was, in his coach's words, "the team's hardest worker—the first guy out to practice and the last to leave." His diligence paid off. By his senior year, Namath, now a broad-shouldered, 6-foot-1, 195-pounder, emerged as a top-flight schoolboy signal-caller. His splendid passing—he completed 84 of 120 passes that year—and dazzling running propelled Beaver Falls to its first state championship in 35 years. Suddenly, Joe Namath was a star. He would remain one for a long time.

Joe's heroics made him a hot item to college recruiters, who were competing not only with themselves, but also with major league baseball scouts. A graceful, power-hitting outfielder, Joe batted .450 and displayed all the tools of a blue-chip pro prospect. Football, however, was his first love. He elected to pursue his career at the University of Alabama, one of the top football powers in the nation.

It proved a wise decision. Directing a devastating offense, Namath bloomed into an All-American. Experts marveled at his shotgun arm and lightning-quick release. Time and again, he would wait until the last possible moment, defenders swarming about him, and just like that, he would snap off a bullet downfield. He could throw bombs with uncanny accuracy, dropping 50-yard missiles right into the arms of streaking receivers. And he exhibited the soft touch of an artist at the short-passing game. His swift, elusive running made him a great two-way threat. That is, until a fateful day against North Carolina State.

Rolling out to look for a target, Joe twisted one way and his knee went the other. The knee buckled, and Namath collapsed in agony. A couple of weeks later he wrenched it again. He had surgery in the offseason to repair it, but knees, perhaps the most fragile part of the body, are not forgiving. Even good knees have a hard time standing up to the pounding they absorb on the football field. Joe Namath was never the same again. The agile cuts and dashing scrambles he used to make routinely were physically impossible. His mobility became greatly restricted. Throbbing pain shot through his legs relentlessly. Namath had no choice; from that point on, he would be strictly a drop-back passer—or no passer at all.

A lot of people thought Werblin had a gimpy brain, offering $400,000 to a quarterback with such gimpy knees. And it was a big gamble, without a doubt. How would Namath hold up in the punishing pro game? What would happen when he was blind-sided by a blitzing linebacker or safety, or sacked by a hulking lineman? Nobody knew. All Werblin and the Jets knew was that they loved his golden arm, and they were convinced it could take them a long way if the knees held up. They were right.

Joe the Jet took off from the start. He fired for 2,250 yards and 15 touchdowns and captured Rookie-of-the-Year honors. He also captured the hearts of the New York fans, who fell in love with his aggressive, go-for-broke style of quarterbacking. Usually rookie quarterbacks are timid, unsure of the defensive formations and afraid of making mistakes. But Namath was a game-breaker from the moment he hobbled onto the field. He made mistakes, sure, but he also lit up the fans with excitement and established himself as one of the most dangerous passing threats around.

He improved rapidly, and so did the Jets. In 1966, he led the league in passes, 471; completions, 232; and yardage, 3,379; and ignited the young team to a 6–6–2 finish. Broadway Joe, they were beginning to call him, and he almost always put on a terrific show.

In 1967, gimpy knees and all, Namath rolled up 26 TD tosses and 4,007 passing yards, more than any quarterback in history. With every game, he seemed to mature as a play-caller and reader of defenses. His mind worked every bit as fast as his rifle arm, detecting defensive weaknesses and taking good advantage of them. With Namath at the helm, the Jets quickly emerged as one of the most explosive teams in football. More conservative quarterbacks completed a higher percentage of their passes and usually had fewer interceptions. But none could match Namath in going for the big strike and putting points on the board in a hurry. Broadway Joe was a game-breaker without peer.

"There are two factors in judging a quarterback: preparing for him, and playing him," related one coach. "Joe Namath scares you both times. When you play the Jets, your whole ap-

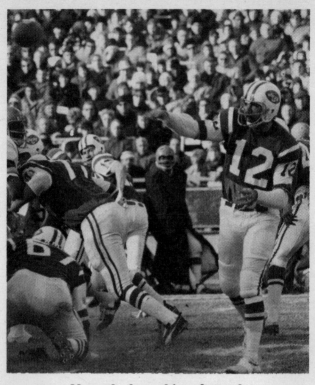

Namath shows his soft touch.

proach to the game involves him. You're con-
scious of him; it disrupts your plans. In the game,
no matter what the down or distance, he's capable
of hitting a big play on you.''

The Oakland Raiders found that out the hard
way. They led the Jets, 23–20, late in the 1968
AFL championship game. Time was short. On

their own 32, the Jets had a long way to go and little time to do it. Dropping back in the pocket, Namath threaded a 10-yard completion to split end George Sauer. Joe took the snap and faded back once more. Fleet flanker Don Maynard was streaking down the sideline. Namath cranked up and launched a pass that traveled nearly 70 yards in the air. It settled right into Maynard's waiting hands at the Oakland six-yard line. One pass later—a TD bullet to Maynard—and there was joy in Jetville. In only 55 seconds, Joe Willie had moved his team 68 yards—and into the Super Bowl showdown with the Colts. The AFL's MVP in 1968 didn't do too badly on that occasion either.

Though nothing could match the thrill and drama of his showing in Super Bowl III, Joe continued to be a stellar performer for years to come. After being sidelined with injuries for most of 1970 and 1971, he returned with a flourish in 1972, firing for a league-leading 2,816 yards and 19 touchdowns. Six of those came in one game. Many people think it was the finest passing exhibition of all time.

On one side was Namath, on the other the great John Unitas, Joe's boyhood idol and the longtime standout for the Colts. The two master slingers came out firing and never let up. Unitas's numbers were staggering. He connected on a career-high 26 completions, for 376 yards. Namath's were even better. His 15 completions accounted for 496 yards—an astonishing average of 33 yards per pass. Of his six TD's, four were for 65 yards or more. In one 89-second span, Joe drilled three scoring strikes, all against a deep-dropping zone that was designed to deny Namath the long pass.

Dazzling as Namath was, he was surrounded by a rapidly deteriorating team. When the Jets struggled to a 3–11 finish in 1976, it was obvious the team needed an overhaul. "And I'm too old to be in a rebuilding program," said Joe at age 33. He was right. It made no sense to send Joe out with a band of rookies and untested players. The quarterback and the team agreed it was best to part company. Joe signed with the Los Angeles Rams, where he stayed only one year before retiring. The Rams were looking for a younger, more mobile quarterback to direct their offense, and after 13 seasons of having his creaky knees banged up, Namath certainly did not fill the bill.

The name Joe William Namath won't be found alongside as many records as some other quarterbacks. And it's true, as his critics are quick to point out—flashy and outspoken, he was no stranger to criticism—that he did not lead his team to a consistently high rate of success. But it's equally true that not even a bold, explosive quarterback can overcome a team's deficiencies in other areas. "Joe is Napoleon without an army," said writer Larry Merchant, "and every week he has to take Moscow." The truth is that through most of his career, Namath played on so-so teams, and he did superbly to take the Jets as far as he did. As Don Maynard once observed, "Joe is so great he makes up for weaknesses we may have in other spots."

Other quarterbacks have had higher completion percentages, fewer interceptions, and higher ratings. Joe's gambling style of play did not lend itself to league-leading statistics in those categories. But few other quarterbacks came close to Broadway Joe in their impact on the game or in their ability to ransack a defense with bullets, bombs, and a passing skill that was beautiful to behold. He took over a decrepit, deficit-ridden team and showed them how to win. He stirred up interest, made people want to come and see him play, and led an entire league, teetering on the brink of collapse, out of trouble and into prosperity.

But perhaps his most memorable feat of all came on an overcast day in January, 1969. That was when he picked apart one of the greatest defensive teams of all time; when he won a Super Bowl championship and a Most Valuable Player trophy with one of the finest clutch efforts by any quarterback ever; when he made good on the most outrageous prediction the football world had ever heard.

"Only Joe Namath would've made that guarantee," said one writer. "And quite likely, only Joe Namath could've backed it up."

Joe Willie braces for a jump pass.

JOE NAMATH

Year	Atts.	Comps.	Pct.	Yds.	Tds.	Ints.
1965	340	164	48.2	2220	18	15
1966	471	232	49.3	3379	19	27
1967	491	258	52.5	4007	26	28
1968	380	187	49.2	3147	15	17
1969	361	185	51.2	2734	19	17
1970	179	90	50.3	1259	5	12
1971	59	28	47.5	537	5	6
1972	324	162	50.0	2816	19	21
1973	133	68	51.1	966	5	6
1974	361	191	52.9	2616	20	22
1975	326	157	48.2	2286	15	28
1976	230	114	49.6	1090	4	16
1977	107	50	46.7	606	3	5
Totals	**3762**	**1886**	**50.1**	**27,663**	**173**	**220**

O.J.
SIMPSON

It was a snowy, wintry Sunday in New York, and all eyes in the football world were riveted there. Not because the matchup between the Buffalo Bills and New York Jets meant anything in the standings. Not because it was the last regular-season contest and a playoff spot was hanging in the balance.

The only reason fans everywhere were following the game so intently was because of a single player and his single quest. His name was O.J. Simpson, and his quest was a record long-considered as untouchable as a record can be. Going into the final game of the 1973 season, the acrobatic running back had piled up 1,803 rushing yards. He needed only 61 yards against the Jets to eclipse Jim Brown's mark of 1,863 yards.

O.J. got his record-breaking campaign off and winging in the very first game of the season, breaking loose for 250 yards against the New England Patriots. Four consecutive outings of 100 yards plus put his total, through only five games, at 813 yards. The talk began. "Simpson's on a record-breaking pace. Can he keep it up?" Defenses keyed on him, and coaches tried to devise special formations to stop him. Nothing worked for very long. At 6-foot-1 and 212 pounds, Simpson was as elusive and graceful as any ball carrier in history. He was a master at the instant stop and start, at stutter-stepping a defender into a frozen position, then blazing right by him.

After dashing for 157 yards against the Kansas City Chiefs in game seven, O.J. surpassed the 1,000-yard mark, a milestone most backs would love to achieve in a full season, let alone half. But as he proved with dazzling certainty every week, he was not like most backs. The pressure mounted as the season moved on. The opposition became even more intent on shutting him down. Through 12 games, his total stood at 1,582 yards. With only two games to go, Simpson had to gather close to 300 yards to beat Brown. A slight slack in his pace in the second half of the season had left his chase of Jim Brown's record in a precarious position. Any shot at reaching the 2,000 mark—a longtime dream of O.J.'s—seemed beyond all hope.

Until game No. 13, that is. Dashing through the snow in Buffalo's Rich Stadium, Simpson picked up 219 yards against the Patriots on only 21 carries. O.J.'s arsenal of fakes and cuts made the New England defenders look like they were playing on a field of grease. Orenthal James

Juice hurdles past a defender.

Simpson—''Juice'' for short—now was not only knocking on Jim Brown's door, he was only 63 yards away from passing through it.

The Bills were fired up for the season's finale. Especially the offensive line, a runner's best friends, and the men who had been opening holes for O.J. all year long. They called themselves

"The Electric Company" because they "turn the Juice loose," and they were ready to light up the Jets. "We'll get it," vowed offensive guard Reggie McKenzie in speaking of the record. "We'll get it if we have to run Juice 64 times."

O.J. wasn't thrilled with the snowy New York weather. "When I saw the snow, I felt bad," he said. "But then I remembered it snowed the week before in Buffalo, and everything turned out okay." Quarterback Joe Ferguson handed off to his star back early and often, and it was immediately clear the snow wasn't going to stop O.J. from making his appointed yards. Again and again, he slashed through the Jets defense, dodging would-be tacklers and gaining good yardage. Late in the first quarter, he slipped through an opening and went for six yards and a new NFL record. The carry pushed his total to 1,864 yards. Simpson had done it, but it was no time for fanfare. Running the way he was this day, he had revived hopes of reaching 2,000.

The Electric Company kept moving the Jets off the line, and O.J. kept finding daylight. As the fourth quarter began, he needed only 60 yards. Ferguson kept in close touch with coaches on the sidelines to keep track of how much Simpson had to go.

The drama built as time ticked away. Juice squeezed out 21 yards on a Buffalo drive, but the New York defense stiffened. The Bills punted. Loud, long boos sounded through Shea Stadium. Even the Jet's fans were pulling for O.J., who was always among the most popular athletes of his time.

Buffalo's defense held the Jets, and the Bills and O.J. got the ball back. Taking a hand-off, he juked inside and turned the corner, springing free for a 22-yard pickup. A crack up the middle got him nothing, but on the following play O.J. took off around left end for nine more yards. Ferguson's on-the-spot computation revealed there were only eight yards to go.

Two plays in a row, the quarterback sent fullback Jim Braxton into the middle. The boos welled up again, but Ferguson knew exactly what he was doing. The man needed a little breather. The next play was O.J.'s, and he took off left once more, good for five. So far, his total for the day was 193. His total for the season was 1,996.

The Bills huddled, and Ferguson called for play 5, designed for O.J. to follow Braxton through the middle. Joe took the snap. Braxton plowed ahead, clearing a path in his wake. O.J. tucked the ball into his midsection, and off he went. He spotted a hole and slid into it in a split second. He slipped through for seven yards before being hauled down. Almost before he could pick himself up, Simpson was swamped by the entire Buffalo team. O.J. Simpson had done it! He'd gained 2,000 yards (2,003 to be exact) in a single season! A thunderous ovation filled Shea Stadium. "Was that hole big enough for you?" beamed Braxton. His teammates carried O.J. triumphantly to the sidelines, where he hugged his coach, Lou Saban. Later, the only member of the 2,000-yard club gratefully acknowledged the support he got from his teammates. At a postgame press conference, O.J. insisted the Bill's entire offensive unit join him so they, too, could take a turn in the spotlight.

"I want to introduce the guys who've done the job for me all year," said the humble record-breaker. "It's their record as much as mine." O.J. introduced each of them individually. His thoughtfulness meant a lot to his teammates.

"He's one heck of a man," said McKenzie, the offensive guard. "I mean, who else do you know would take the entire line to a national press conference the way he did? He's just beautiful. The man is the greatest in the world at what he does. That's number one. But number two, the man does not dish out any jive. He doesn't brush off people who aren't stars, who don't start."

Simpson's record-shattering feat would've meant a great deal to him under any circumstances, but it gave him added satisfaction because of the way his pro career began.

The first player selected in the 1969 college draft, O.J. came to Buffalo after a glittering career at the University of Southern California. In only two seasons (previously he went to a junior college) at USC, Simpson ran up the staggering totals of 3,124 yards and 35 touchdowns. It was a foregone conclusion that he would be the Bills' selection. Indeed, the Bills's 1–12–1 record the year before was the envy of a lot of teams; by being so pitiful, they'd insured themselves of the top pick—an athlete who was being hailed as a once-in-a-generation running back.

People had sky-high expectations of swift No. 32. Rushing titles, 1000-yard seasons, winning football—all this and more was being looked forward to by the hungry fans of the western New York city. They were disappointed when things didn't pan out that way.

Right from the outset, O.J. encountered a lot of difficulty in Buffalo. Foremost was the fact that the Bills were a team of two distinct factions; in one corner were the holdovers from the franchise's glory years, when the team was a powerhouse in the American Football League. In the other were rookies and newcomers. Another problem was that the coach, John Rauch, didn't think a back could be effective in the pros running the ball 25 or 30 or more times per game. The coach felt that would make it too easy for the defenses to key in on a back. Simpson felt very much differently. He wanted the ball, and he wanted it a lot. The more runs he got, the more he felt in the flow of the game. "Let me run," declared the rookie, "and I'll make Buffalo a winner."

O.J. didn't run much, the Bills didn't win much, and nobody was very happy. For another runner, gaining 697 yards as a rookie would be quite an accomplishment. For O.J. Simpson, the most heralded first-year back in league history, it was quite a disappointment. A knee injury interrupted his second season, and in 1971, the situation for all concerned got even worse. Under new coach Harvey Johnson, Buffalo slipped to 1–13, the worst mark in the league. Juice, who was misused, underused, and simmering with frustration, felt like his career was going sour. With three seasons under his belt, he had yet to perform the way he knew he could. There were words around that Simpson was a flop, a runner who seemed to peak in college and who couldn't sustain that success as a pro. Simpson heard the talk, and he didn't like it one bit. He insisted his confidence was unshaken and that he was the same swift and slippery breakaway threat he had always been. The trouble, he maintained, started and stopped with Buffalo's failure to give him a steady diet of carries. All he wanted was that chance. In 1972, he got it.

With no place to go but up, the Bills rehired Lou Saban, the coach who had directed them to prominence in the 1960s. One of the new coach's first initiatives was to seek out the Juice. "We know you're a great running back," Saban told him, "and we're going to give you the ball as often as we can." Having constructed a potent running attack in his first tenure with the Bills, Saban set out to do it again. He implemented new plays and acquired some fresh blood for the offensive line.

The difference was like night and day. The Bills didn't set the league afire with their 4–9–1 record, but they no longer were pushovers and had taken significant steps in the right direction. And Simpson? He finally was the O.J. people had watched in awe at USC. Getting the ball far more than he ever had before as a pro, O.J. responded by amassing 1,251 yards and capturing his first league rushing title. In his first three seasons, he had managed only three 100-yard games. In 1972 alone, he had six. He was a reborn runner, dashing and darting and slipping and sliding, shredding defenses with moves only he could make.

The 1973 season was O.J.'s record-breaker, in more ways than one. Apart from his mark of

The snow couldn't stop O.J.—neither could the Jets.

2,003 yards gained, his breakthroughs included: most yards gained, game, 250 (a record he surpassed in 1976, when he ran for 273 yards in a game); most consecutive games, 100 or more yards rushing, season, 7; most games, 100 or more yards rushing, season, 11; most games, 200 or more yards rushing, season, 3; and most consecutive games, 200 or more yards rushing, 2. On top of it all, he averaged the remarkable figure of six yards every time he carried the ball.

Neither O.J. nor anybody else has been able to duplicate his wondrous achievements of that 1973 season. But that's not to say Juice didn't do a lot more dazzling before retiring in 1979. Twice honored (1973 and 1975) as *The Sporting News* Player of the Year, he ran up five straight 1,000-yard seasons, including 1,817 in 1975, when he established still another record by scoring 23 touchdowns. He followed that by piling up 1,503 more yards in 1976, picking up his fourth NFL rushing crown in the process.

At that point, O.J. was less than 3,000 yards away from surpassing Jim Brown's career rushing total of 12,312 yards. Even if he failed to maintain the spectacular pace of his previous seasons, Simpson seemed a shoo-in to supplant Brown as the most prolific rusher in NFL history. It was a record O.J. dearly wanted. He made that clear. He also made it clear he wouldn't prolong his career just for the sake of having his name alongside a record. He wanted football fans to remember his agile artistry as a runner. "The thing is," he said once, "I want to leave the game like Jim Brown—who quit while he was still the best."

The record never came. A knee injury intervened in 1977 and in his final two years, spent with the San Francisco 49ers (a San Francisco native, O.J. wanted to wind up his career in his hometown, and the Bills granted his wishes), it was clear he was not the Juice of old. He simply was unable to recapture the magical moves that, for most of the 1970s, made him the most dangerous running threat in football.

Record or not, O.J. Simpson remains the standard by which halfbacks are judged. His graceful sprints and slashing cuts gave him a running style that was like poetry in motion.

When O.J. was a youngster, he and his friends used to hang around Kezar Stadium, hoping to run into the pro stars. Once, after a game between the 49ers and the Cleveland Browns, one star emerged from the locker room and ran into the group. His name was Jim Brown, and he'd just rushed for 135 yards and two touchdowns against the 49ers.

"The other kids were really awed," O.J. said with a grin. "But you know, I was the leader of the gang, so I had to say something.

"Jim Brown, you're not so great," said O.J., laughing now at his youthful brashness. "When I get to play pro ball, I'm going to break all your records."

Brown was quiet. "You talk big now," said the Cleveland great, "but let's see what you do when you get the chance."

"Now kids are always coming up to me just like that and saying they're going to break all *my* records," O.J. went on. "So I tell them what Jim Brown told me."

O.J. Simpson paused. Then he added, "The fact is, someday somebody will."

Another fact is that the someday another running back does what O.J. Simpson did one snowy Sunday in New York may be a long, long way off.

O.J. SIMPSON

Year	Atts.	Yds.	Avg.	Tds.
1969	181	697	3.9	5
1970	120	488	4.1	5
1971	183	742	4.1	5
1972	292	1251	4.3	6
1973	332	2003	6.0	12
1974	270	1125	4.2	4
1975	329	1817	5.5	23
1976	290	1503	5.2	9
1977	126	557	4.4	0
1978	161	593	3.7	3
1979	120	460	3.8	3
Totals	2404	11,236	4.7	75

DAN
FOUTS

Dan Fouts's childhood was a boy's dream come true. Most kids would give anything just to get an autograph from an NFL star or to watch a pro football clash from a front-row seat. When he was ten, Dan got to do much more than that. The son of the play-by-play announcer for the San Francisco 49ers, he got a job as the team's ball boy, which allowed him to be right on the field and gave him a chance to talk and joke around with the 49ers—sometimes even play football with them. For these thrills, Dan didn't have to give up anything. All he had to do was chase down errant footballs.

The nicest fringe benefit of all, though, was getting pointers from the pros on the proper techniques for basic football moves. What better place to learn? The 49ers had men like Y.A. Tittle, John Brodie, and Billy Kilmer as quarterbacks—all NFL standouts—and he took valuable tips from each of them. Obviously, Daniel Francis Fouts was an exceptional student.

Maybe Dan's experiences had nothing to do with the fact that he wound up plying the same trade as his boyhood heroes. Maybe he would've gone on to be a spectacular, record-breaking quarterback anyway. He says he had no clue then that he would follow in the footsteps of Brodie and company. "I was so young, football just seemed like a bunch of older men doing something," said Dan. "I really never dreamed I'd be playing pro football myself. It looked impossible." The San Diego Chargers, the high-powered team he directs, are certainly glad he changed his perspective.

For some four years running, the 6-3, 205-pounder has been playing a game that might be called "Fouts Chases Fouts." Because that's exactly what he has been doing. He sets a record, he breaks it; he sets a record, and breaks that, too. There has to be some limit to what Fouts can accomplish. It's just that nobody knows what it is.

Quarterbacking life hasn't always been so rosy for him. Though he led his high school team to a league championship, his efforts were overshadowed by those of Jesse Freitas, a rival signal-caller who, ironically, later played with the Chargers, too. (Freitas had the good fortune to have as a receiver an acrobatic young man named Lynn Swann.) The recruiters didn't trample each other trying to lure Fouts to their school. In fact, only one college—the University of Oregon—

offered him a scholarship. He accepted and headed for the Pacific Northwest.

It was there that Dan first fell into the record-breaking habit. By the time he left Oregon, he'd logged an impressive pile of achievements, including 5,995 passing yards, 37 touchdowns, and 19 school records. He was hardly a household name because Oregon wasn't a football school that commanded much attention. But he was eventually noticed by those who mattered; the Chargers selected him on the third round of the 1973 college draft. Five quarterbacks were tabbed before him: Bert Jones, Joe Ferguson, Ron Jaworski, Gary Huff, and Gary Keithley. Which just goes to show that even the most knowledgeable football people, who spend thousands of hours watching games and studying films, can't always accurately judge a player's potential.

Joining the Chargers, Dan found himself a mentor in aging great Johnny Unitas, who closed out his career in San Diego. "I tried to emulate him," said Dan. "I went to him for advice and for a shoulder to cry on." There was a lot to cry about. A franchise in ruins, the Chargers had about as much order as a department store on the day before Christmas. They went through six offensive coordinators in seven years, plus several head coaches to boot. Adjusting to pro football is hard enough for a young quarterback without that kind of turmoil swirling about him.

The Chargers were hapless, and Fouts was practically helpless. He had almost no protection from his offensive line, absorbing, week in and week out, as much punishment as any quarterback in the league. His reward was to be unmercifully booed by the San Diego fans, who were exasperated rooting for a perennial loser.

The situation didn't improve until 1976, when the great coach, Bill Walsh, became offensive coordinator. Seeing much untapped potential in the young quarterback, Walsh worked closely with Dan and instituted a much more pass-oriented offense for him to work with. Fouts responded by having his finest season as a pro, connecting on 58 percent of his passes for 2,535 yards and 14 touchdowns. San Diego won six games, which wasn't great, but was a lot better than the year before, when it won only two. For the first time in years, a glimmer of hope appeared on the Chargers' horizon.

With a rapidly maturing Fouts at the helm, that glimmer soon emerged as full-fledged radiance. After sitting out a good chunk of the 1977 campaign because of a contract dispute, Dan led the team to nine victories in 1978. His performance, which resulted in a completion mark of 59 percent, 2999 yards, and 24 touchdowns, was one of the two prime factors for San Diego's best showing in ten years. The other was Coach Don Coryell, who took over early in the 1978 season. An expert in the passing game, Coryell laid out his intricate offensive system and Fouts made it work. The two were an ideal match. "He's a genius," said Fouts of his new coach. "Do you know we're averaging six yards per snap? No one knows more about moving the football than he does. He sees things in defenses no one else does. He probes defenses with subtle things like putting people in motion, seeing how they react. He doesn't ask players to do things they physically can't do. He's a perfectionist. He puts great emphasis on success on every snap."

The admiration is mutual. "We're only doing what we do because of Dan," the coach praised. "He has such a flexible mind. He doesn't have all the qualities you'd want in an ideal quarterback. He's not a runner. He's a fine athlete, but he doesn't have the speed. But he is very, very intelligent, and he is extremely competitive and tough mentally. Our passing game is very complex, and Dan has to be able to tell every player exactly what to do on every play. He does that extremely well."

Before long the high-flying San Diego offense became known as "Air Coryell," and Fouts was its incomparable pilot. In engineering the team to a 12–4 finish in 1979, Fouts fired for more

Dan scans the field for a target.

yards—4,082—than any passer in history. He did it by completing better than 62 percent of his passes, good for 24 touchdowns. He also set a mark by throwing for 300 or more yards in four consecutive games. To the surprise of nobody, he was voted the league's Most Valuable Player.

Ever since, Fouts has spent most of his time rewriting the record books. He surpassed his 1979 performance in 1980, and established still more marks in 1981, when he had what many experts believe was the finest year of any quarterback ever to play. He attempted a record 609 passes, completed a record 360 (a 59 percent completion pace), for a record 4,802 yards. He also drilled 33 touchdown passes. "There are a lot of good quarterbacks in the NFL," said Coryell. "But I would not trade the one I've got."

What makes Fouts's success all the more remarkable is that he isn't as naturally gifted as many other signal-callers. He's a classic overachiever. He doesn't have the arm of a Bradshaw or a Namath, and he can't run the way Staubach could. What he does have is an exceptional passing touch and an uncanny ability to find an open target anywhere on the field, even when he's about to be engulfed by some mountain man on the opposing line.

But Fouts's greatest asset of all may be his guts. In a game loaded with tough players, he is among the toughest. Played out hundreds of times over the years, this scene came in a game against the Seattle Seahawks: Dropping back to pass in a tight contest, Fouts stands in against a fierce blitz, waiting until the last possible moment to release an artful 49-yard strike. He gets popped hard and winds up on his back. The Chargers get a touchdown. It's a trade-off Dan Fouts will make any time.

"Fouts is so tough, so very tough," said Joe Gibbs, a former San Diego assistant who coached the Washington Redskins to the Super Bowl in 1983. "And I think he imparts that toughness to the rest of the team. They see he'll do anything to win, and they go out there and play the same way."

"He's a leader," added Bob Klein, a former San Diego tight end. "He may not have the best arm in the league, but he makes up for it with his brains. And he's tough. He'll walk up to anybody on the line—some big lineman—and tell him to get his show on the road if he's not doing his job." But if they do their jobs, Fouts is the first to congratulate them. "He's one quarterback who doesn't have a big ego," said one teammate. After games, Fouts and the offensive line go out to dinner. If Dan has gotten sacked that day, the blockers pick up his tab. If he hasn't, Dan forks over for them. It's probably the one time when he's only too happy to be paying the bill.

Never has there been a better showcase of Fouts's character than in San Diego's memorable 1981 playoff thriller against the Miami Dolphins. Dan's final line in the game was awesome: 53 passes, 33 completions, 433 yards. Chalk up three more records for the bearded former ball boy. He played even better than his stats showed.

After watching his team fritter away a 24–0 lead, Dan led the offense on with under five minutes to play, San Diego trailing 38–31. If he didn't put seven points on the board in a hurry, the Chargers' season would be history. Cool and courageous, Dan picked apart the Miami secondary with the precision of a surgeon. Swiftly, his pinpoint passes moved San Diego to the Miami nine. Dropping back once more, he spotted running back James Brooks in the clear. He fired. Touchdown! The score knotted at 38, the duel

Fouts breaks a record with practically every pass.

went into sudden-death overtime. The first team to score would win.

Dan pushed his team to the doorstep of victory early in the extra session, passing superbly to advance the Chargers 79 yards. Rolf Benirschke came on. All he had to do was kick a 27-yard field goal. Usually automatic from that range, Benirschke's boot sailed wide. The drive was for naught. The Dolphins had life. Momentum swung in their favor.

Undaunted by the disappointment, the battle-weary Fouts brought this team storming back the next chance he got. A few of Dan's drillers and San Diego was on the charge again. Fouts faded back from the Miami 49. Charlie Joiner blazed down the sideline and quickly veered deep over the middle. Fouts delivered a strike to the gifted receiver, the 39-yard connection going to the 10-yard line. Benirschke trotted on once more, a precious chance to be pardoned. This time the task was a 29-yarder. The ball was snapped and held cleanly. Benirschke stepped up and hit it squarely. There wasn't any doubt. The kick was good. The longest game in pro football history was over, and the Chargers came away the victors.

Fabulous to the end, Fouts called it "the greatest game I've ever played in." It's a wonder he had the strength to call it anything at all. He lost ten pounds in the heavy, humid Miami air. Bloodied, battered, and caked with dirt from the four-hour epic, he trudged off the field as though each step might be his last.

"I've never seen a display of passing and courage like that," raved Sid Luckman, a former NFL great and Hall-of-Fame quarterback. "Fouts was unbelievable. If he's not the best to ever play—and I'm not sure he isn't—he's got a chance to be before he's finished."

"Awesome" was the adjective used by Joiner. "No other quarterback ever has done more for his team. He is phenomenal, the best in the league."

About the sole remaining challenge for Dan Fouts is to lead the San Diego Chargers to a Super Bowl championship. Individually, he has accomplished every goal imaginable. His name is all over the NFL record books. He is the single-season record-holder for attempts, completions, and yardage. He has thrown for 300 or more yards in more games (30) than any quarterback in history. He is the only man ever to lead the NFL in passing for three consecutive years. He is second to Ken Stabler in career completion percentage (58.2) and is closing in on lots of other marks. Odds are good that before he retires he'll have them, too.

Still, the ultimate triumph has eluded him, and

fierce competitor that he is, Dan Fouts won't feel complete until he's wearing a Super Bowl ring. "Athletes nowadays are always talking about themselves," said Dan. "But football is a team game. The satisfaction comes in winning, and that's not an individual thing. . . . All I've accomplished means nothing. Individual records and accomplishments are great, but I'd trade every record and every stat for a Super Bowl title."

A childhood dream came true for Dan Fouts, the ball boy. Maybe, for Dan Fouts, the quarterback, an adulthood dream will come true, too.

DAN FOUTS

Year	Atts.	Comps.	Pct.	Yds.	Tds.	Ints.
1973	194	87	44.8	1126	6	13
1974	237	115	48.5	1732	8	13
1975	195	106	54.4	1396	2	10
1976	359	208	57.9	2535	14	15
1977	109	69	83.3	869	4	6
1978	381	224	58.8	2999	24	20
1979	530	332	62.6	4082	24	24
1980	589	348	59.1	4715	30	24
1981	609	360	59.1	4802	33	17
1982	330	204	61.8	2889	17	11
Totals	3533	2053	58.1	27,145	162	153